151

Quick Ideas

to
Inspire
Your Staff

By Jerry R. Wilson, CSP

CAREER
PRESS
Franklin Lakes, NJ

151 Quick Ideas to Inspire Your Staff
Edited by Jodi Brandon
Typeset by Christopher Carolei
Cover design by The Visual Group
Printed in the U.S.A. by Book-mart Press

To order this title, please call toll-free 1-800-CAREER-1 (NJ and Canada: 201-848-0310) to order using VISA or MasterCard, or for further information on books from Career Press.

The Career Press, Inc., 3 Tice Road, PO Box 687,
Franklin Lakes, NJ 07417
www.careerpress.com

Library of Congress Cataloging-in-Publication Data
Wilson, Jerry R., 1944-2005
151 quick ideas to inspire your staff / by Jerry R. Wilson.
    p. cm.
Includes index.
ISBN 1-56414-829-7 paper
1. Employee motivation. I. Title: One hundred fifty one quick ideas to inspire your staff. II. Title: One hundred and fifty one quick ideas to inspire your staff. III. Title.

HF5549.5.M63W56 2005
658.31'4--dc22

2005052637

Contents

Foreword

Getting more done faster and with better results are the objectives of corporations today around the world. What is it that makes one company excel and another exist? *It is the competitive edge*—the edge that is found in Jerry Wilson's *151 Quick Ideas to Inspire Your Staff*. Its practical, hard-hitting ideas and examples are both relevant and necessary in business today. This is the book that will give you the edge. It's the book that you don't want your competition to read!

Jerry's book offers a treasury of ideas that are immediately usable, actionable, and profitable and that were forged and proven on the battlefields of business competition. Throughout the book and in a variety of ways, Jerry delivers his core message again and again: "Your staff will be no better than the people you hire and the inspiration you give them."

Another of Jerry Wilson's truths that underlies this book is about why people do what they do:

Inspiring people is about getting other
people to do, what you want done,
because they want to do it.

Leadership is about creating the climate or culture where people are inspired from the inside out. Inspired employees want to see their organization succeed, because it will also lead them to their own personal successes. That is the winning formula: inspiring ordinary people to achieve extraordinary outcomes. *151 Quick Ideas to Inspire Your Staff* provides us with the winning strategies that lead employees to that level of commitment.

As you read this book you will discover quick ideas from a man who speaks from experience, not theory. Jerry proved these ideas in his own successful business ventures. In addition, they have been tested and proven by thousands of business and professional people following Jerry's professional presentations to audiences across the United States and Canada, and in numerous foreign countries.

151 Quick Ideas to Inspire Your Staff will recharge your battery and excite you, as Jerry has provided not only what to do, but also how to do it. You will be ready and able to inspire your people to give their individual best. You will gain the proper mindset, have the right tools, and be able to practice effective techniques from this treasure trove of good ideas. Jerry taught thousands of people his enthusiastic, inspiring and authentic quick ideas to inspire others—and now it is your turn! Read the book and watch your visions become reality.

Thanks, Jerry!

SteveHanes
The Dale Carnegie Course

How to Use This Book

Every quick idea in this book has been selected to directly or indirectly help you gain and retain customers, create relationships, and build a successful business.

Don't try to implement all 151 ideas at once, because some won't be a good fit right now. Read through all 151 quick ideas and select only those that can really make a difference. Label your ideas:

- Implement now.
- Review again in 30 days.
- Pass the idea along to _____.

Involve your staff in selecting and implementing these ideas, and don't forget to give credit for their success! Invest in additional copies of this book and distribute them among your staff. Get everyone involved in selecting and recommending various quick ideas.

Revisit this book every 90 days. As your business changes, you will find new quick ideas that might suit you better now that competition is heating up.

Remember: All the ideas in this book have been proven in businesses across the United States and around the world. They have worked for others and will work for you!

1

Work on, Not in, Your Business

There's one fact that can truly be labeled a blinding flash of the obvious if you're sincere about improving your business. If you wait to have time, you'll never get around to it. Some law of nature always fills our agenda. Practicing *kaizen* and continuous improvement means you must make time to work on, not just in, your business. You will never have time if you don't *make* the time.

Jack was always too busy working to rethink marketing strategies and to be cultivating potential customers. No amount of pleading by his sales staff could get him away from operations. He believed the company would always have a steady flow of work. When their largest customer defected to a competitor, Jack was faced with making a mad scramble to replace the work or be faced with laying off many of his quality workers that he would probably never get back.

Assignment

On a 3 × 5 card, posted above your desk somewhere you will see it every time you sit down, write: "I will work on my business—and my team—today."

It's easy to overlook needed improvement today, and it's almost certain you'll look back in time and say, "I wish I had...," "I should have...," and "Why didn't I...?" as they'll become part of your conversation— part of the "coulda, woulda, shoulda" routine.

Epilogue

Procrastination robs us of a valuable commodity: time. Today is the day to begin improving and practicing kaizen.

2

A Better Way to Think, Feel, and Act

Kaizen is the Japanese word for the philosophy of daily incremental improvement—the practice of each day finding small improvements that can add up to long-term quantum leaps for improved quality, productivity, processes, and so forth. For this assignment we look for a quantum leap in the way you think, feel, and act.

When you listen to businesspeople discuss what is going on with their jobs, their companies, or their leadership, you'll almost always hear them talking about their *activities*. Why do we constantly bat around this talk about our activities? Experts tell us it is largely because it gives us good feelings to know we have been busy, and therefore we think and feel we are being productive.

Assignment

On a 3 × 5 card in large bold letters write down: "OUTCOMES!" Then below that bold word add the following sentence: "Customers want to know W.I.I.F.T. (what's in it for them)!"

Can you find me even one prospect or customer who cares about the activities, the busywork, and what goes on inside your firm or organization? What do customers care about? Outcomes, and what is in it for them. In other words, they couldn't care less about your labor pains; they simply want you to show them the baby.

Epilogue

Think outcomes, and you'll soon find your organization embracing the practice of incremental daily improvement.

3

IASM

It is said that life is a series of ongoing challenges interrupted by a periodic crisis. How true that has proven to be! It is true that everyone in business faces setbacks, roadblocks, and bouts of occasional discouragement. Good leadership means learning to minimize those challenges and crises, but to also develop an internal persistence to work through them.

When Mary Kay Ash founded Mary Kay Cosmetics, with little money and the challenge of being an unexpected widow, she needed a secret weapon to persevere with her dream of helping others succeed with her in her startup cosmetics business. Her answer was to become so sold on her products and her unique business opportunity that she and others could visualize the big

Assignment

On a 3 × 5 card write out the top three things you are sold on as it relates to your products and services, and how they benefit your customers. Use these key talking points to continuously remind yourself and your employees as to why you have the initials IASM as top of mind.

bold letters *IASM* (*I Am Sold Myself*) emblazoned across their chests.

As she grew Mary Kay Cosmetics from a startup vision into an international success story, she never gave up the belief that to overcome the challenges and crises that everyone faces, you must be absolutely sold on your products and services. Being absolutely, positively sold leads to the persistence and tenacity needed to persevere.

Epilogue

It is how you respond to what happens to you that will keep you going when others give up.

4

We Care and You Matter

It is difficult if not impossible to find a business that doesn't claim to care about its people and to hear how much they matter to the organization's success. They say it, they put it up on signs and banners, and they brag about how they care and their people matter to anyone who will listen. The problem is that to really inspire your staff means that you must both say it and *live* it.

When a Minneapolis-based company was forced to reorganize under Chapter 11 bankruptcy, one of the new practices they thought would inspire their embattled staff was to offer cash rewards for good ideas and suggestions. One of the first to take advantage of the offer looked at his $50 suggestion reward check and asked a very telling question. *Why*, he asked, *when you were going broke did you not seem to care about me and my ideas, and now that we are in bankruptcy I not only matter but you are willing to pay me for my ideas?* Ouch!

Want a simple and meaningful way to prove to your people that you care and that they matter? Execute the assignment at right and you'll not only be rewarded with a more inspired crew, you'll gain tons of great ideas and feedback to help you grow and improve.

Assignment

On a 3 × 5 card, write the word "ASK" again and again. And below it add: "People don't care how much you know until they know how much they care." Then, routinely ask your people for suggestions—and act on those suggestions when you get them.

Epilogue

You can shout you care from the rooftops and you can put up signs and banners about how much your people matter, but what will inspire them is when you demonstrate it.

5

Your Job Is All About THEM

Sometime over the years you have heard the great debate about which came first: the chicken or the egg? A second debate has been which comes first: your customers or your staff? After much discussion, debate, and research, my vote is that your staff must come first if you want to grow beyond yourself and to multiply yourself through other people.

The late W. Clement Stone became one of America's first billionaires by inspiring hundreds and then thousands of sales and management people to join him in growing his Combined Insurance Company into an industry giant. One of his key success methods was to live and breathe the principle that you will get what you want when you help enough other people get what they want.

He served as a role model and inspiration for many business leaders as he reminded them that the only way to get people back on track when they lose their way is to go back to their individual goals, dreams, and aspirations.

Assignment

On a 3 × 5 card write down the following introspective question to ask yourself about your people again and again: "Do I *really know* what each of my people wants as his or her individual benefit of being part of helping me build and grow this business?" Put this card at the start of a file section that will include cards on all of your employees.

Epilogue

Nothing can pay off more than knowing what your people want from you and their work, and then helping them achieve it.

6

The "Why" Is What Everyone Overlooks

Young children are masters at asking the "why" question. In fact, many a parent has been driven to the edge of insanity as kids ask "why" in an effort to understand and deal with their world. Just because you are trying to inspire mostly "big people," from perhaps teens to senior citizens, doesn't mean inquiring minds have lost the need to know why.

Consider the plight of Sue as her understaffed and overworked library staff filed into the library conference room for an unexplained but mandatory meeting. Sue was faced with telling her staff that they were about to endure a year of living hell as the town council had voted to not only double the size of the library, but to renovate and remodel the aging facility as well.

> ### Assignment
>
> On a 3 × 5 card, write out a minimum of three answers as to "why" you are excited about the future of your company and the opportunities for your staff to grow and prosper with you. Then begin incorporating such "why" dialogue to go along with the requests you ask of your people.

With that announcement would come the reality that the year ahead would be filled with noise, dirt, moving, hassles, and ongoing upheavals too numerous to even think about.

Fortunately, Sue was smart enough to focus her announcement on the "why" of the situation, rather than the challenges ahead. As her crew learned why libraries had to change to keep up with the public's demand for more Internet-based services, as well as more space for training and learning, they caught Sue's vision and were inspired to look to the future of a bigger and better facility.

Epilogue

Become proactive in telling "why" when it is important, and watch your people respond with new vigor and inspiration.

7

Creating Your Magnet Story

At some time in your life you have had the opportunity to see or use a magnet and to see what appears to be almost magic as the magnet is attracted to metal. It may be as simple as those holding notes on your refrigerator door, or as big and complex as the giant magnet at the end of a crane boom that can lift huge piles of metal and scrap. Now, you need such a magnet to attract and inspire people to join you and your company.

Look at volunteer organizations and how people are not only attracted to serving, but how they do it for nothing and even pay their own expenses. Why people volunteer and how so many organizations such as United Way and the American Red Cross attract people is the essence of this idea.

Go back to the first day you founded your company, or the day you took over from someone else. What was the story behind that decision that attracted you? What was the deciding factor and driving force that went beyond money to inspire you to make that decision? What was the compelling force that got you to take that leap of faith?

Assignment

On a 3 × 5 card write out the answers to these key questions:

- ◆ How does your company "directly" benefit others with your products and services?

- ◆ What personal story can you tell that shows why you feel good about what your company does to make the world a better place?

- ◆ What is your magnet story about what you are doing to help others by solving problems, improving things, and making others dreams come true?

Epilogue

Define your story in such a way that it will attract people the way a magnet does.

8

Your Job: To Sell Again and Again and Again

Advertisers measure the number of "repetitions" as the number of times they must reach you with the same message in an effort to inspire you to buy their clients' products and services. Ad agencies know that just when you get sick and tired of seeing the same commercial over and over, they are getting to you and building "top of mind" for the products and services they are attempting to sell you.

The same is true with selling your workers on the merits of working for you. You have to make impression after impression to sell them on the merits of your company. One TV or radio ad is very unlikely to inspire you to run out and buy the latest and greatest new product. Likewise, telling and selling your company to your employees demands selling your story again and again and again.

> ### Assignment
>
> At the top of a page of paper begin writing down all the opportunities you have and need in order to sell your message again. From written communications, to meetings, to daily conversations, you must realize a big part of your job description is to sell your own people. Making a long list will help you keep it "top of mind awareness." Then, convert the top 10 opportunities to a 3 × 5 card and post where you can see it every day to remind you to sell.

> **Epilogue**
> *When you get sick and tired of the same message, your staff is probably just beginning to get it.*

Steal, Don't Invent, Your Success

Every successful leader needs a mental data bank of business principles, good ideas, and competitive strategies from which to make good decisions to help them sort through the many choices facing them each day. One early choice to make is whether you are going to be an inventor, pioneer, or thief.

As Thomas Edison did, you can spend your days in painstaking, expensive, and time-consuming experimentation. You can do trial and error and spend your career groping for answers, or you can join me in stealing good ideas that work.

Today the phrase *best practices* has become the buzz in companies to seek out the best ways and methods for doing things and for making decisions. Let me suggest you steal your best practices from proven successful people. Also, look outside your profession, occupation, or field for the best ones.

> ### *Assignment*
>
> On a 3 × 5 card capture this quote to review again and again: "Find out what successful people do, do what they do, and you too will be successful."

For example, if you want to model best practices for operating multiple locations, look to McDonalds. For cleanliness, UPS is the perfect model. For consistency, learn how FedEx keeps its promises of overnight delivery. The list can go on and on.

Epilogue

There are a ton of want-to-be and claim-to-be people who try to look successful. Limit your research to folks who have truly "been there and done that."

10

No Man Can Serve Two Masters

The Bible repeatedly points out that "no man can serve two masters." You know what that means biblically, but how should you apply the lesson in business? Confucius said it another way: "Man who chases two rabbits, catches none."

Study successful Japanese companies, many of which have been around for hundreds of years, and you'll find they have committed themselves to one master: serving the customer. Companies such as Toyota, Suzuki, and Yamaha know that the customer must come first and profits will follow. In fact, many Japanese businesspeople practice the philosophy that profits are the applause of happy customers.

Examine how successful Japanese companies have moved into areas thought sacred to American companies and, over time, have kicked their butts. Probably the best example is how they captured market share in auto sales by delivering on quality, safety, and fuel economy. They put the customer first, and the profits have followed.

Why must your commitment to customers come first? If your focus is on profits and the bottom line, then your decision-making will also follow that model. Your first critical thinking will be weighed through your bank account and may not be what is best to gain and retain customers.

> **Assignment**
>
> On a 3 × 5, card write out this reminder: "No man can serve two masters. For me and my employees, we will serve customers first, foremost, and always."

> **Epilogue**
> *Are you committed to serving one master: your customers?*

11

Teamwork

You need only look to the U.S. military to find the ultimate successful model for implementing teamwork. After 200 years the military knows what works, and teamwork is the only model the U.S. military will consider. You play on the team or you are gone. No discussions, no debates, and no verbal fistfights.

Look at our elite fighting units, such the Navy Seals or the Army Rangers, and you have your teamwork model. These special units live and breathe an "all for one and one for all" philosophy in everything they do. They know that anything less is a waste of time and energy for getting things done.

Dennis, a Florida attorney, owned three small retail stores that were just doing "okay." Then he heard a quote about teamwork that changed his total approach to business: "First you build the team, then the team builds the business."

From that day on, Dennis focused his efforts on selecting, training, inspiring and leading his team. Then he got out of the way and empowered the team to build the business. When his family sold out to a larger company the team efforts had propelled them from three "okay" stores to more than 500 stores and financial success beyond anyone's wildest dreams.

Assignment

On a 3 × 5 card note these three guiding teamwork principles:

1. Success is a team sport!
2. Teamwork means "Together Everyone Accomplishes More."
3. First you build the team, then the team builds the business.

Epilogue

For more guidance in creating teamwork and turning your business into a team sport, there is no better resource than studying the U.S. military.

12

Be Demanding: Setting Your Standards

"People want to be told what to do and will do what they are told." That quote is an ever-present reminder that even as adults we need leadership, direction, and boundaries. And one of the best things you can do for your team is to be a demanding boss.

Not a boss that yells, screams, and dictates orders. And no, not a boss who sees his workers as slaves, subjects, or people he or she can dump on. The best description of a demanding boss is someone who lives "friendly but firm." A "steady as she goes" leader guides and directs his or her group toward their best performance. Best performance comes when everyone understands what the standard for good performance is for your organization.

Being a demanding boss means being specific without compromise. For example, be demanding that you will answer the phone on or before the third ring. Your group will return all voice mail calls by 4 p.m. You can be demanding that your group will under-promise and over-deliver.

Assignment

On a 3 × 5 card note your commitments: "I will be a demanding boss and live the friendly but firm principle for setting my standards."

Epilogue

Keep your friendly but firm compass on what is important to customers, and everything else will fall into place.

13

Turning Every Worker Into a CRM

Job descriptions are important, but most have a bad, if not fatal, flaw. By listing the common job description it provides an escape hole for employees to miss their responsibility in building customer relationships and repeat business. If you are totally sold on the concept of serving and creating long-term customer relationships, then each and every person in your organization should share in that commitment.

When a visitor at Disney World watched a cast member, one of the performers, stop and pick up some litter and deposit it in the trash can, she asked her tour guide how many custodians they have. The answer: 45,000. And how many employees are there at DisneyWorld? The same answer: 45,000. Everyone at Disney has a shared purpose in maintaining the park's image. From the boiler room to the boardroom it is a sense of unity that makes the Disney magic work.

> ### Assignment
>
> On 3 × 5 card write out new job descriptions with the title CRM—Customer Relationship Manager—listed first. Under that, list their other important titles, which comes second to the CRM issue.

Do all of your staff members see themselves as part of the most important thing you do—that is, creating customer relationships? If so, great! If not, consider this important job of inspiring them to join you in this effort, just as Disney folks have joined together to keep the park sparkling clean. Both job descriptions lead to repeat business.

Epilogue
One deadly phrase all too prevalent in companies and organizations is "it's not my job."

14

What We Expect of You

I can tell one thing about each and every one of your co-workers, employees, or associates: Each of them has many good attributes, but one thing they can't do is read your mind! They need you to tell them what you expect of them so they can meet or exceed your expectations.

Ever work for a boss or supervisor who didn't tell you what to do and then criticized and chewed on you for not doing it? How about the boss who doles out orders the way an Army Drill Sergeant does but fails to tell you the outcome he or she wants and expects of you? How does it feel to attempt to do your work while playing mind games with your boss?

To be inspired at your work demands that you have a sense of satisfaction and accomplishment. How can you create that sense of well-being if management treats you like a mushroom to grow in a dark

---

Assignment

On a 3 × 5 card write out up to 10 things you expect of your employees in doing their jobs. Then use this list, titled *"What I Expect of You,"* in your hiring, reviews, job postings, meetings, award ceremonies, and so forth.

29

environment? What does your leadership expect of you as it relates to attitude, honesty, work ethic, productivity, integrity, teamwork, and such?

Epilogue

By putting your employee expectations in writing, you will be rewarded with a much happier, more productive, and incredibly more loyal workforce.

15

Don't Compete With Yourself

Who is your prime competition? It isn't who you are about to name. My suggestion is that to recognize and deal with your number-one competitor, look in a mirror. It is probably you!

Consider the plight of an insurance company that bought a similar company, one of its competitors. The staff in the company it purchased believed they were better at nearly everything they did and, when the new owners suggested changes, improvements, and attempts to standardize how the two companies would work together, the new company rebelled. It was a daily battle of wills, politics, power, and personalities.

If you and everyone in your company were doing everything you know, plan and want, your competition would be nonexistent. If you consistently delivered your products and services to exceed customer expectations every time they dealt with you, your competition wouldn't have a chance. If every person on your team was inspired to do his or her very best every day in every way, how could your competition compete with you? Fact: you may well be your own number-one competitor.

30

Assignment

One a 3 × 5 card list the issues and things that are problems today that are distracting you and your workforce from giving 100 percent attention to your customers. How are you shooting yourself in the foot? Where and how are you creating your own problems, distractions, and work that isn't productive?

Now gather your staff together and have them list who they perceive to be your company's competitors. Then use your list and this topic to introduce that you are your own number-one competitor and that beginning immediately that is going to change. You are going to drive out those glitches, problems, and inconsistencies.

Epilogue

Make a vow to let your competitors be your competitors and do everything you can to not be your own competition.

16

Too Soon Old and Too Late Schmart

My grandfather was an immigrant from Europe, and his favorite saying from the old country was "you will be too soon old and too late schmart." The extra "ch" reflected his broken English, but his message was clear and concise.

When it comes to inspiring people he firmly believed that the challenge was so great and the many situations one faces are so daunting that everyone needs to look to others for input and direction. He was constantly reminding anyone who would listen that two heads are better than one, and that when we talk we only learn what we already know. When we ask and listen, we learn and grow.

How many people do you work with, lunch with, go to church with, and encounter in your business life that have and are willing to share their good ideas about inspiring people and leadership strategies with you? Surely dozens, and perhaps hundreds. And all you need to do is develop the habit of asking and listening!

Assignment

On a 3 × 5 card write down my grandfathers favorite saying: "You will be too soon old and too late schmart." Then accept my challenge of keeping that card visible to remind you to ask, ask, and ask some more. In fact, make a commitment right now to memorize this powerful management tool: "What do you think I should do?" It may be the most potent tool a leader can develop!

Epilogue

The world belongs to the askers, who can make you look good and inspire your troops!

17

Mother Teresa's Advice

Living a life of selfless service and helping others isn't easy, but with practice and a commitment it can be done. The feelings you gain in helping others are the bonus payoff. However, one person described it as being more challenging than nailing Jell-O to a tree.

To guide you in doing a better job in selfless service we picked Mother Teresa as a role model. In fact, she could be our inspiration number 1, number 2, and number 3. She dedicated her simple life to building her missions and to rescuing the sick and dying from the streets of Calcutta, India. Her goal was to allow people who were lost to die with dignity in an environment of love

Assignment

On a 3 × 5 card, record the last time someone—a customer, perhaps—thanked you sincerely and personally for helping him or her. Date the entry. Think about how you could get more of those entries. Set out to get one entry a day—then two—then three. Start your employees doing this as well. Have them make their own cards. Remember: the words *thank you* are the currency of helping people. Set an eventual goal of using up at least one 3 × 5 card per day recording these events.

and caring, unselfishly served by her nuns, who she called her angels.

Her best quote to inspire us is this: "You will find yourself when you lose yourself in service to mankind." How would you rate Mother Teresa's commitment to serving? How would you rate your commitment to serving and helping others? Are you getting that second paycheck in those feelings that inspire you and others on a daily basis?

> ### Epilogue
> *Always remember that people whom you help today, will come back to you for more help tomorrow!*

18

1-2-3 Is Your Job Description

People who live their faith, values, and principles want to work with other people with the same commitment. General Norman Schwarzkopf said, "People want to be lead by leaders who have more integrity than they do." Mary Kay Ash, founder of the Mary Kay Cosmetics empire, taught her 1-2-3 System for living a life of meaning. First, she described herself as a woman of faith. Then she lived, taught, and preached to others to follow her model, and her thousands of employees and sales associates were constantly reminded of her commitment: God first, family second, and job third.

One good example of very successful companies that demonstrate their 1-2-3 approach is the chain of Hobby Lobby stores and the rapidly expanding Chick-Fil-A restaurants, both of which close on Sundays so their families can worship. They demonstrate their beliefs by putting aside sales, money, and profits to live their philosophy.

Assignment

Do you have a 1-2-3 system? If not, develop one. On a 3 × 5 card, write down your first, second, and third priorities in life. Do they look right to you? If so, post them somewhere to remind you what they are. Then, communicate theses priorities to your team. They want to know you are principled and have priorities.

Epilogue

Apply Mary Kay's 1-2-3 System in your life and you will be more inspired, and thus be able to better inspire others.

19

Answer the WHY Questions: Your Company

When you were a child, perhaps 2, 3, or 4 years old, you had one favorite question: WHY? It seems every child uses the why question and often drives parents to near insanity. Inquiring minds want to know *why*.

When Don, who is responsible for a Georgia manufacturing plant, was faced with temporarily laying off about 80 workers, his first decision was to go to the plant and tell them why.

He assembled everybody in the lunchroom and explained that in an effort to revamp the plant and make it more productive so they could compete, they were going to need to shut down for a period about nine weeks, and thus about 80 people would be laid off. He went on to explain that it was part of the company's long-range plan to provide better jobs and higher productivity, and thus be able to pay everyone more. He apologized for having to lay people off, and at the end of his briefing the people who were about to be laid off applauded.

Adults still want to know why but often have become too jaded or inhibited, or are afraid to ask. We lose those childlike inhibitions of asking why.

Assignment

On a 3 × 5 card, write the statement: "Tell them why." Review this card before making major decisions that will affect employees.

Epilogue

People want to know why about corporate policies and the direction of their work. And when you fill in that needed information you will be rewarded with people who are more excited, motivated, and inspired.

20

Answer the WHY Questions: Your Employees

When your employees ask why they should be inspired to make your company more successful, your answer should always focus on one simple answer. By making the company more success-ful, you can be more com-petitive and do a better job of gaining and retaining cus-tomers, which in turn allows you the resources and the opportunities to inspire, rec-ognize, and better reward your workforce.

When a major insurance company wanted to grow, they knew it was imperative that the entire company be staffed by competent em-ployees. They found that by answering the why question, competence builds confidence. There are three major components to building confidence:

1. **Experience.** They go through the battles, mis-takes, and problems they face on a daily basis.

2. **Knowledge.** They inspire their employees to be a part of a lifelong learning experience.

3. **Success.** Nothing builds competence the way vic-tories and successful outcomes do.

> ### Epilogue
> *Growing people is not quick, easy, or without effort. You should start with the end result—that competence builds confidence—in mind.*

21

How to Park Your Ego

On several occasions in this book we'll point out the need to get yourself out of the way and practice what many call "selfless service." You already know that putting aside your personal and selfish motives isn't easy.

Gary was a cut-from-the-cloth entrepreneur. He was driven, persistent, and relentless in his plan to make his retail stores a huge success and financial payoff. When I arrived to consult with him the only thing he had been able to accomplish was to really upset his workforce and to make himself borderline insane.

As I worked with Gary, the problem with his leadership style leaped out of every sentence, every interaction, and every conversation with his workers. It was the deadly "I" message: *I* want you to do this. *I* want you to fix this. *I* want you to…. I, I, I. He sounded like a 2- or 3-year-old we expect to be caught up in the "I want" syndrome.

What Gary had to do was rethink his leadership style and realize that at the end of the day people do things for their reasons, not yours. As Gary began to study and learn this important truth he made a 3 × 5 card that I recommend you duplicate for your daily review.

Assignment

On a 3 × 5 card, write out the word "ego" and then draw a circle around it. Then place a left to right slash through the word "ego" at a 45-degree angle as we would use to indicate no smoking. Each time you review that card, think about each of your people and what they want and need from you to do their jobs well. It will be different for each and every person, and the list will change as people, situations, and needs get filled and changed.

Next, write down or memorize this quote: "The secret of leadership is to get other people to do what you want done, *because they want to do it.*"

Epilogue

The secret is to park your ego and appeal to theirs.

22

Own Their Head, Heart, and Soul

Certainly you have heard the phrase "hook, line and sinker." That truism probably came from fishing and dragging that big one up on the bank. Your goal should be to "hook" your associates, employees, and management by capturing their heads, their hearts, and their souls. To make a connection so deep and so profound that even thinking about defecting to another job with someone else presents extreme risk and a great, big helping of gut-wrenching guilt.

A university study found that when you use logic and facts about your salary and benefits, you connect with people's intellect. They found that when you use emotions and feelings you connect with their heart, but to connect with their soul you need to be more profound. You need to connect with them on a personal level. The best way to do that is by adding stories about the positive experiences that they will enjoy from your customer relationships.

> ### Assignment
>
> On a 3 × 5 card, write down some of the emotional "hooks" that you could use with both employees and customers. Some of them are simply emotional wins, failures, and so on. ABC Sports coined the phrase "the thrill of victory and the agony of defeat." Start there.

Make everything you do targeted to hooking up with the soul. Your team needs to feel this way 24/7.

> **Epilogue**
>
> *Raise the bar and look for ways to get them "hook, line, and sinker," or by their heads, hearts, and souls.*

23

Who Gets the Credit?

An important principle for inspiring people is to "give credit where credit is due." Although that is easy to say, in practice many people find they seem to lose a small piece of their souls when they put others in the spotlight.

When Harry asked for the opportunity to re-work a section of our high-performance department, it felt that I was giving away a member of the family. That was my sacred responsibility and the mere thought that anyone else might invade my turf really was a struggle. But his eagerness to try it, and my having to admit the area needed an update and attention, got him a green light.

Harry did an awesome job. That department had never looked so good, and we now had a resident display expert available for our entire store.

> ### Assignment
>
> On a 3 × 5 card, record this core principle for inspiring people: "There is no limit to what people can accomplish if they don't care who gets the credit." Next, list some people and accomplishments you need to recognize for their accomplishments. Update this card as needed. Start today to teach yourself to be better at sharing the credit where credit is due.

41

It turned out to be a triple win. First, with Harry eager and ready to use his newly proven skills, I was free to focus on other things. Second, Harry had proven that, given the chance, we can do more than expected, and this was a lesson to his coworkers. Third, Harry's self-confidence took a quantum leap and he was inspired from the inside out.

Epilogue

Learning the principle of "praising in public and correcting in private" may not come naturally or easy to you. But the payoff of having a crew who will climb tall buildings and tread across broken glass for you can only come from growing others.

24

Catalog and Use Those Tribal Stories

Down through history we've used various methods to preserve and maintain important lessons and examples that can educate and inspire others. One method used by Native American Indians was story-telling, and some even carved totem poles as visual records of some of their most important lessons to be passed down to other tribe members.

After completing a Cleveland workshop where the focus was teaching the concept of probing and asking questions to determine customers' potential needs and sales opportunities by gaining a "mind picture" of what they were doing, one of the attendees immediately captured and used the technique. While servicing his first customer the day after the workshop, one attendee turned an $8 sale into more than $400 in purchases when he learned the customer had additional needs that he wasn't aware his company could also provide.

This savvy business manager quickly turned this sales experience into a tribal story. First, he sent an e-mail to all employees telling the story and bragging about this person. Then he made some posters to go up in their break rooms recounting this heroic effort. In addition, he added a module to their training program so they could use this victory story again and again. He was determined to use this tribal story repeatedly as a powerful teaching tool.

Assignment

Start a file of 3 × 5 cards with tribal stories of heroics and situations where your staff went "above and beyond" to serve, sell, and help customers. Everyone loves and can relate to stories, and they can act as a real tool to inspire and motivate others to action.

Epilogue

Everyone needs heroes and heroic stories and, as you collect your library of successes among your tribe, you can begin to integrate them into your training, reminders, and examples to lead and inspire others.

25

If You Have Time to Lean...

One thing every manager must face is his or her role in making sure his or her people are as productive as possible, and that everyone contributes his or her best to the company's success. If you have people standing around with nothing to do, payroll cost is likely to break you. For most companies, payroll cost is their number-one expense and one of the few variables that can make or break a company.

Ray Kroc, founder of McDonalds, coined the saying, "If you have time to lean, you have time to clean." In short, he knew that keeping everyone working and using their spare time to keep every McDonalds restaurant spotlessly clean and sparkling was necessity for the company's success.

Can you afford to have people standing around looking out the window waiting for the next phone call or customer contact? To maximize your success you need everyone making a contribution every hour of the day. Controlling payroll costs and maximizing productivity of all your workers is job number one for management. Take a cue from Ray Kroc. Make sure your people are focused on making the most of their time and your payroll expense.

> ### *Assignment*
>
> Each day, post a short list of things that need to be done on a 3 × 5 card in the event your people get caught up with their jobs. When there is an ever-present list, no one can say they didn't know what needs to be done. Take away their excuses with a new general duty list posted each and every day.

Epilogue

*Your peak workloads should be when there are no cus-
tomers waiting and the phones are quiet. Now is the time to
get ready for that next surge of business.*

26

Roadblocks and Resources

Perhaps you thought this book was going to be all about
how to inspire and motivate your employees. But it is really
about changing how you lead. It's about helping you identify
the mistakes you have been making so you can move into a
new style of operating. It is about taking on a new way of
thinking and acting so you can get the outcome you want.

One savvy executive claims to think of himself as a Roto-
Rooter man. He sees his employees as working in a long drain-
ing tube, and his job is to flush out everything that clogs up the
flow. If you don't, you're not adding real value. It is your team's
responsibility to do your job with excellence. It is your job to
create an environment that allows your people to be super-
stars. You must do anything and everything you can to allow
them to do their jobs—to truly empower them.

As long as obstacles and roadblocks are placed in the path
of employee success, you will have frustrated and unfulfilled
employees. Your job is to root out those roadblocks and smooth
the way. In addition, always look for resources your team needs
for success, but does not currently have. Find ways to gain
those resources. Then watch how fast employees succeed when
they realize you are helping them succeed!

45

Assignment

On a pair of 3 × 5 cards, write the following headings: "Roadblocks" and "Resources." Discuss internal processes with your team to discover what roadblocks they routinely encounter and what assets or resources they need to be more effective and/or productive. Record these on your two cards. Then, using the cards as your attack plan, work to remove obstacles and gain those resources. Set a goal of accomplishing all of them within a reasonable period (perhaps a month). Celebrate with your team each accomplishment.

Epilogue

Your job is to remove the obstacles and give your people the resources they need and inspire them to get the work done. Then get out of their way!

27

On Message: Your Brand Promise

In years past, businesses used terms such as *differentiation*, *unique selling proposition*, and *niche* to organize and plan how they would gain and retain market share. Then, as competition became more sophisticated and software helped business leaders better define their strategies, the need for developing a brand identity became the voice of defining competitive market forces.

When four young men arrived at their class several minutes late they told the teacher they were late because their car had a flat tire. The teacher, wise to these stories, instructed each to pull out a piece of paper and write down which tire went flat. Guess how many different answers she received? The challenge for every business is to craft a memorable message and to make sure every person is telling the same story every time.

Assignment

On a 3 × 5 card, write down your organization's brand image and promise (what you want your customers to think of you). Now, make every employee make a copy of that card and keep it with them at all times. Quiz them on it routinely. They help communicate your brand with every word to a customer.

You must not only define what sets you apart from the competition, but also "stay on message" to tell and sell it repeatedly. The test is: "What does your brand promise and message mean in the mind of your customer?" This also helps employees more strongly identify with the organization.

Examples: Bounty is the "quicker picker-upper" and FedEx is used "when it positively has to be there overnight."

Ask yourself if your Brand Promise:

1. Truly reflects who you are, what you do, and what the benefits to your customers are.

2. What your customers want and need from you.

3. What sets you apart from competition.

Epilogue

The goal is to promise what you will deliver and to deliver what you promise.

28

A Blinding Flash:
You Are in the People Business

Would you like to join a really exclusive, private, and little-known group of business leaders? An organization that perhaps only 5 percent of all businesspeople in the world ever participate in? If so, here is your opportunity to join my "people business" club.

What business are you really in? When Matt first answered that question his answer was all too typical: He described the dozen locations his company occupied and their history in a very competitive retail service environment. But as he went on to describe their marginal profits and high employee turnover problems, the lights began to come on for Matt. He was really in the people business and just happened to provide the products and services he was describing.

What business are you really in? If you say anything other than the people business, listen to the words of Lee Iacocca, the executive who saved Chrysler Corporation from disaster: "We are in the people business. We build our cars and trucks for people. We work with people, we communicate with people, and we sell to people. If someone working for me isn't good with people, they probably won't make it at Chrysler!"

Assignment

On a 3 × 5 card, write the following: "I am in the people business. My business is about people helping people." Review this card once every day and before every hiring decision.

Epilogue

If you are going to spend your life in the people business—and you are—decide today to become an SOB (student of the business).

29

You Will NEVER Understand People

Every time you take the wrong road you'll end up in the wrong place. One of the most dangerous roads that leaders take is trying to truly understand what motivates and inspires people deep down inside. We must realize that everyone was made different. We are unique individuals, from our DNA to the hairs on our heads.

One wise professor said that you will never understand people beyond a superficial level. Unless you are a psychologist and have them lay on the couch, you can only watch their actions, their behavior, and the results that they get, but you will never be able to read their minds. His favorite quote was, "You must accept people as they are, not as you want them to be." Have you ever watched someone who seemed to be happy and suddenly he quits his job, dumps his spouse, or totally changes his life and you can't understand it? We will never understand people beyond a superficial level.

So what does this mean for motivating people? It means you must take them at face value and judge by what you see, and you must understand that every employee is different, motivated by different impulses, ideas, and emotions.

Assignment

On a set of 3 × 5 cards (one per employee), write down, as best you can, what you think will motivate that employee best. Modify each card as you learn more about them. Then, refer to these cards as you work with each employee to get the most from him or her.

Epilogue

Instead of getting frustrated and confused by the differences you witness in your people, step back and see and appreciate them for their uniqueness, their differences, and what inspires them.

30

Nobody Notices Normal

In today's over-communicated and cluttered world, being "normal" means you are in for a tough battle to get customers to notice and remember you. There are too many "normal" competitors on the landscape. To break through the normal mindset requires being "noticeably different" and at the same time "comfortably familiar."

In Japan the last item on a McDonalds menu board, after the normal burgers, fries, and beverages list, is "smiles - zero yen." And as the sign says, when McDonalds order-takers greet you, they do the traditional Japanese bow, then they flash a gi-ant-sized smile and ask to take your order. Contrast that to all too many service situations today where you are darn lucky if the clerk even makes eye contact or does anything more than grunt.

Look for the hundreds of large and small ways you can get people to notice and remember you by breaking with tradition to be "noticeably different."

Assignment

On a 3 × 5 card, record the "nobody notices normal" mission statement of being "noticably different" and at the same time "comfortably familiar." Begin with challenging your coworkers to identify and implement things that people will notice and re-member. Look at each and every interaction you have with customers as opportuni-ties to set yourself apart from competition. Find and imple-ment at least one idea a week. Reward the employee who developed the idea. Record each idea.

> **Epilogue**
>
> *Be forewarned that being too different can be outside a customer's comfort zone.*

31

Critical First Impressions

Study after study has proven that the first 30 to 90 days a new employee is with you is the most critical time period of that employee's tenure. In fact, the first hours and days may be more important than anyone knows. Here is a simple and effective way you can inspire and impress upon a new hire that you care and they matter to you.

When Brian said yes to joining a professional accounting firm as his first job after college he was hopeful he had made the right choice of employers. But he also was reminded of numerous past jobs that turned out to be disappointing as they related to the promises made to him during the interview and hiring process. He was painfully reminded that in nearly every case his first impressions and first days were disappointing.

Imagine Brian's surprise when the day after agreeing to join his new company a package arrived via overnight courier. Inside was a welcome letter from

> **Assignment**
>
> Poll your coworkers and brainstorm what might be in your new-hire first impressions kit. You don't have to be an international company or a mega-employer to make those critical first impressions. Then create that kit and use it with every new hire.

his new employer, a color booklet describing his new company and its colorful history, some articles highlighting some of its recent notable accomplishments, and—the real winner—a nice company shirt complete with logo in Brian's size and favorite color. He was confident he had made the right choice.

Epilogue

The critical issue of first impressions is to reinforce the principle that you care and they matter.

32

Hire Winners and Fire Your Losers—But Do It Right

Look at the books, seminars, and research on hiring and firing and you'll find the vast majority, perhaps as much as 80 percent, is targeted to the hiring process. Part of inspiring and leading people means that you will at times have to say goodbye to people. Here is some valuable insight into that gut-wrenching process.

Dick, a seasoned business executive and consultant with great insight, made one critical observation about the firing process. He said that if you have any compassion at all, then firing someone is the most difficult any businessperson faces...and that you are a jerk if you enjoy it. Enjoy it or not, here are some cautionary notes about letting someone go.

When you fire someone you are sending a huge message to any and all existing personnel. If in their minds the person deserved being terminated, you are okay. If anyone thinks otherwise, you may have trouble.

If you answered these three questions with yes, go ahead. If not, you haven't done enough yet.

Assignment

Write this lithium test on a 3 × 5 card *before* you fire:

1. Have we made it absolutely, positively, and unequivocally clear this person is going to be fired if he or she doesn't respond to improve his or her performance?

2. Have we asked for this person's help in correcting his or her sub-standard performance? You must get a yes, and he or she must have a willing spirit.

3. Have we offered our help to do our part in helping him or her?

Epilogue

Sometimes one can be faulted for trying too hard to salvage people and fire too late. Cut the dead wood. They are holding you and your team back.

33

The "Must" Checklist

Taking a new job is always going to generate some anxiety, which is an outward expression of fear. The more you can do from day one to reduce that anxiety and make a new person feel safe, the quicker he or she will settle in and be inspired to do a good job.

One California company developed what it called the "Must" Checklist. What that really stood for was things a new employee *must know* to be able to function properly, get along with other people, and know what to do from the first day he or she joined the company. That checklist covered everything from where to park your car to how to find the bathrooms. It reviewed work hours, break times, lunch arrangements, and when payday is. Every new hire received an organizational chart and was talked to about the chain of command.

> ### Assignment
>
> On some 3 × 5 cards, make a "Must" Checklist for the things you believe a new hire must know to be successful in your company. Use that checklist every time someone comes to work, and the payoff will be an employee who is motivated, feels safe, and inspired to be part of your team.

The list dealt with who to ask when you have a question or a problem and went through every must bit of information that they could brainstorm. When a new hire came in, he or she simply started down the list, and by the end of the first day that person was well oriented—probably knowing more about that company than one learns in the first 60 days going to work elsewhere.

> ### Epilogue
> *By taking a proactive approach with new employees, you will overcome their fear to ask.*

34

Invest in People

Two important words in the English language can determine if you are going to grow people and give them the opportunity to maximize their individual abilities, or take the traditional path of just getting by and tolerating less than spectacular performance: *cost* and *invest*.

Assignment

Effective today, be careful about how you label what you spend on growing people. When you discuss anything regarding education, training, and resources for your people be clear to let them know you are making an investment in them. Review your individual 3 × 5 cards on each employee (and what motivates them). Write down how you will invest in them during the coming year.

When Sharon was invited by her boss to attend a three-day nursing conference in a distant city she was flattered and thrilled. Though the thoughts of getting some time off, an airplane trip, and enjoying a motel and the free food were nice, the real impact was that her boss valued her enough to invest in her and her continued education.

If you see training, learning, and resources to help your people as an expense, you'll probably be too cheap to grow people. If you see training, learning, and resources to help your people as an investment that can pay off in many ways, you'll probably make those investments with a smile and get to experience people at their best.

Epilogue

One boss said he didn't want to invest in his people because "they might get smart and quit." His competitor added the alternative: What if they stay with you and remain ignorant?

35

A Chance to Take a Chance

When an applicant says yes and joins your company or organization, there is only one thing you can and should offer him or her: an opportunity. Perhaps said another way, you are giving them a chance to take a chance that they will succeed. Although you have the responsibility to provide the resources, the roadmap, and the opportunity, his or her real fate and future are in his or her own hands. Responsibility means the choice to choose your response. Choices.

When Brian called Trent into the room, they had had two previous discussions about Trent's failure to follow through on his promises as a new employee. Brian asked him if he knew the definition of responsibility. He said he thought he did, but would like to hear Brian's definition. Brian said responsibility is the ability to choose your response, and he pointed out to Trent that he had dropped the ball repeatedly and, therefore, was leaving the company, but he wanted Trent to know that he had

Assignment

Make sure your employee 3 × 5 cards list the standards and expectations you expect of each person on your team. Record the dates you counseled each. This makes it easier when it's time for someone to go or when it's time to reward someone.

failed in his chance. In other words, he had caused his own demise with their company. He committed suicide and was not murdered.

Epilogue

You can't make people successful! All you can do is create the atmosphere, give them the resources and leadership, and get out of their way, giving them a chance to take a chance.

36

The 3 × 5 Card System Agenda Jogger

Nothing is less expensive that has a better chance of helping you be better at inspiring your people than my key management tool: the 3 × 5 index card. Available most anywhere and at a cost of well less than a penny, the index card can and should be as much a part of your life as the ink pen, car keys, and wallet.

Consider Mike's frustration as, in just one hour, he saw employees failing to offer to help customers to their cars with their purchases, observed another chitchatting with coworkers rather than paying attention to a customer, and another who failed to give the company's number-one commercial: We want you back. All were noted on Mike's 3 × 5 card for later attention.

How many times each day do you encounter a situation, or you observe some-

Assignment

Instead of just forgetting these problems, use a 3 × 5 card to jot down those issues to address later, perhaps in a training meeting or one on one with the people involved. Where you keep this particular index card is not terribly important, as long as it is close by where you can jot down a quick note, reminder, or thought for action at a later date. But remember: A 3 × 5 card with no action taken is a waste of a 3 × 5 card.

thing that you would like done differently, but you lack the time to address or it is too trivial to address at that moment?

Epilogue

Successful leadership is about effectively managing a few big things and 1,000 or more smaller but often critically important little things.

37

Horses and People = Breeding and Past Performance

When selecting people, there are two key ingredients that Dr. Phil and most authorities will recommend you check very thoroughly. One is the past performance of the person you are thinking of hiring, and second is the environment in which he or she has worked over the years with various companies that will determine attitude, work ethic, values, and principles. There is a common parallel with picking quality people and picking racehorses.

Timely Gift came from a Chicago racetrack where it had an unparalleled record of winning. The horse came out of great breeding stock and, as I approached the play window, it was clearly obvious this class horse could not be beaten by the other nags in the race. But be forewarned: Knowing past performance and breeding is no guarantee. My horse ran fourth, and it's the last horse race on which I've ever bet money. I would rather take my chances and bet on people.

> ### *Assignment*
>
> "Past performance and breeding." Write this on a 3 × 5 card. Use this card to prepare for any upcoming job interviews to help remind you to get under the surface and discover the "inner view" of each candidate.

As you explore and interview people, get a clear vision of what they have done in the past. Talk to them about their successes. Have them tell you the things they are proud of. Not hypotheticals, but real-world stuff. Second, wrap yourself around the atmosphere and environment in which they have worked in the past.

Was it high-pressure, intense, or laid back? Did their culture fit yours? All those things become important. To be able to get an "inner view," you need to know what's inside.

Epilogue

You will be no better than the people you hire and the leadership you give them.

38

Discrimination Is Alive and Well

Everyone does it! You do it, I do it, and the president of the United States does it. We discriminate against people. Even though there are numerous federal, state, and local laws, regulations, and rules about discriminating, everyone uses discrimination when it comes to the goal of hiring the best and avoiding the rest.

Robert Yates, one of the great experts on hiring the right people, gives us three questions to guide us when we discriminate as to who we will hire:

Assignment

On a 3 × 5 card, write down the three questions provided here. Use this card during your hiring process to make your best hiring decisions.

1. Is your applicant capable of doing the job?
2. Is your applicant willing to do the job?
3. Is your applicant manageable on the job?

Everything you do in the hiring process, from interviews to background checks, should be focused on answering these three questions. And only if you get a solid yes in all three areas should you go forward to offer a job to a potential candidate.

Epilogue

Even the best hire may not be a fit for your company. He or she may not fit with your culture, with your team, or with your way of doing business.

39

Be a Magnet and Attract the Best

It is a proven fact that the best organizations earn their reputation by offering the best products and services to the best customers. This formula acts as a magnet, allowing them to attract the best workers. This truism has been proven through the ages across the entire spectrum of businesses and organizations.

Doug, a young construction worker, was a bright star in a profession often viewed as being staffed by crusty, rough, and tough workers with long hair, beards, and a chew of tobacco. His eagerness to do quality carpentry work was coupled with a clean-cut, sober, friendly, and trustworthy demeanor. Doug's value was evident to employer after employer, without even looking for a job. He was propelled up the ladder from one company to another and ultimately landed the construction job most of his peers would kill for. The cream always rises to the top.

Reverse this. Set your goal to be "the employer" the best employees want to work for, offering the best training, the best work situation, and the best pay and benefits possible. Sadly, most employers try to practice offering the minimum they can get by with and normally end up with less than spectacular workers.

Assignment

On a 3 × 5 card, list the key attributes for becoming a "best" employer. Examine what you can do—perhaps incrementally—to become that best organization. Create a plan based on the card. Once you begin to achieve this status, then only hire the best.

Epilogue

It takes the best to attract the best, and the place to start is by being the best employer and inspiring the best people to your organization.

40

Hiring Smart Means Never Selling the Job

Show me any employer who has interviewed to fill a job and chances are he or she has been guilty of selling the applicant on taking the job, instead of letting the applicant do the selling and convincing. All too often we spend most of the interview time talking about the job, the company, and not enough time really exploring the applicant's qualifications for the job. Today, commit to flip-flopping those priorities.

Ray was so excited about the company to which he had given birth that every job interview was predictable. Ray would get potential workers so excited and lathered up about joining his team, he totally overlooked issues including qualifications, work ethic, attitudes, and ability to really do the job. It took many years of making bad hires before he realized he had to fit the right person to the right job and that meant asking questions and doing a lot of listening.

Assignment

On a 3 × 5 card, write down this series of exploratory questions to ask every job candidate. Use this card during every interview. Here are some examples:

- Tell me about one of your most significant successes on the job. What made it so significant? How did you accomplish it?

- Tell me about a major problem you handled recently. How was it resolved?

- By using personal examples, show me you can adapt to a wide variety of people, situations and environments.

- Give me an example of an important goal you had set for yourself in the past and tell me how you reached that goal.

- Describe some times when you were not really pleased with your performance. What did you do about it?

Epilogue

If ever there is a time to put a governor on your mouth, it is during the interview process.

41

Invest in Yourself

The president of the Success Foundation, the late Kop Kopmeyer, once sent me what appears to be a stock certificate (similar to what you would receive if you owned stock in a New York Stock Exchange company). It has a nice border around it, and the title is "Your Self Stock Certificate." The text reads:

> This certifies that you own one million shares of stock in yourself. This is your certificate of confidence in yourself and your agreement to begin at once and constantly use 151 quick ideas to get whatever you want as a worthy life goal.

> The best investment you can make is in you. You can make more money or acquire more of whatever you want—by investing in You than in any other investment. Nobody buys stock in anything unless he or she has confidence in it because, in buying educational tools, you really bought stock in yourself. You have proven that you have confidence in yourself.

Now that you have bought stock in yourself and proven that you have confidence in yourself, you have taken the first step in getting whatever you want in life.

If you don't take good care of you and invest in

Assignment

Create your own stock certificate and hang it on the wall in your workspace. ("What, no 3 × 5 card?")

your mental, spiritual, and physical self, you are worthless to anybody else. You are worthless to the ones you love; you are worthless to your spouse or significant other; and you are worthless to your family, friends, and your team of workers. So when you make improvements in yourself, think of it as an investment—the most important investment you will ever make.

Epilogue

Do you take care of the people around you that you care about? Of course you do. So why not invest and take care of yourself?

42

Invest in Your Team

One of my psychology professors talked endlessly about the law of transference, that the only way you can transfer good feelings is when you get good feelings yourself. Here's the way he said it: "You can't give away something you don't have any more than you can come back from someplace you ain't never been." You must take care of the people who take care of you.

If you want the people to take care of your customers, then you need to take care of them. Caring creates caring. Each time you have an interaction with one of your employees, your staff,

---

Assignment

On a set of 3 × 5 cards, write or type clearly and in bold letters the word "*care*." Post this at all points where your team interacts with people (registers, phones, counters, and so forth). Remind your team that you care and they care. That feeling will get passed on by transference. Don't to forget to post one at your desk, too!

or your team, think about how you want them to feel and what feelings you want them to pass on to your customers, and if you treat them in such a way that they have those feelings, you will have instilled the law of transference in them. It almost creates an obligation where they feel guilty if they don't do it.

Epilogue

The Bible repeatedly says, "As you sow, so shall you reap." Reread this quick idea and see how that applies to the principles that make up this quick idea.

43

Invest in Your Customers

Take care of your customers and your customers will take care of you.

Noted motivational speaker Zig Ziglar said it another way: "Help enough other people get what they want, and you will get what you want." Herb Wardlow, who guided Kmart to become America's number-one retailer, long before it got knocked off the pedestal by others, said, "Find out what people want and give it to them." And he added an additional thought: "and then some." In other words, give people

---

Assignment

On a 3 × 5 card (still have a good supply?) write: "Take care of your team and your customers, and they will take care of you." Post it where you can see it every day. You take care of your team, collectively you all take care of customers, and the customers will take care of all of you.

more than they expect, do it willingly, and watch them come back for more.

There's another rule that you can follow in making all of this work to take care of your customers. It's called the platinum rule: "Do unto others as they want to be done unto." If you think about all three of these quotes, it comes to a very simple premise: Find out what people want, help them get it, and then add something to it, and you will have success beyond your wildest expectation.

Epilogue

Take care of your team of workers, and especially take care of your customers, everything else will take care of itself.

44

Give 'Em a Great Reputation

Imagine being an Olympic athlete going out to perform before the eyes of the world. Your reputation and their expectations should inspire you to give your very best on every try. That same priciple can apply to help you inspire your workforce as they do their daily jobs.

Sue was proud to be the supervisor of a team of outstanding office workers and often gave tours to suppliers and competitors from other areas of the country. She was proud to show off their new state-of-the-art office facilities and to explain why her group had such an incredible track record for efficiency and productivity. At each stop she would introduce the person doing a particular job and brag about him or her, telling something about his or her background and what made him or her exceptional. The employees just glowed.

Positive reinforcement of good performances works—especially when it is conducted in front of others.

Assignment

Create a new set of 3 × 5 cards—one for each employee or team member. Record for each at least two positive traits or performance characteristics true for that person. Then, using the cards, make a point of publicly reinforcing these traits through praise at least once each week for each employee. Do it in front of other team members and/or customers.

Epilogue

Make it a habit to brag about your people at each and every opportunity, especially in front of strangers. Watch them perform as though they're Olympic athletes.

45

Can We Be Friends?

The question most often asked of me, as a professional speaker and a consultant, is: "Can you really be friends with your employees and your subordinates?" My answer is yes, but then you have to define what friendship means in your language.

I would like to believe that it is essential to be friends with your employees. Consider this idea: One business owner had a black baseball cap embroidered with two words in gold: The top line said "Friend" and the second line said "Boss." When he took someone aside to have a conference with them about their performance, he would wear that cap. He would start by telling them that he would like to believe that they are friends, but he also had a second job and that was to be their boss. Then he would take the cap off and say this is the time I have to be the boss.

It's important to use the cap because it is so visual. People can see the difference in the two relationships when you reach up to take the cap off.

Assignment

Save your 3 × 5 cards this time. Have a ball cap made with the two words most appropriate to you. Are you a boss, a supervisor, a manager, a department head—and friend?

Epilogue

Your most effective relationships with employees will be personal. You have to be friends with them, but you also have to be the boss.

46

Protect Yourself From Workers With "Selective Memory"

Nothing is more inspiring, encouraging, and motivating than a boss or supervisor who has an uncanny memory to keep his or her promises about dates and agreements to review pay, benefits, and other performance-related issues. And nothing is more demeaning and debilitating than a boss who always seems to develop amnesia and never can remember what they promised or agreed to do.

Every time Mary sat down with Harry to review his pay, performance, and benefits, she was amazed about the differences in what they recalled from previous discussions. It seemed each time that Harry and Mary met, Harry's recall of Mary's promises, terms, and conditions about raises and benefits was always much inflated from what Mary remembered. Finally, Mary decided Harry had a case of "selective memory" and was using their pay and performance discussions as an attempt to take advantage of Mary's forgetfulness and lack of record-keeping.

Assignment

On a 3 × 5 card (yep, one for each employee), record the date of each counseling meeting with each employee and what was agreed/promised by each party at the meeting (what you agreed to and what the employee agreed to). Set a date for the next meeting and record it. Copy the card and provide the copy to the employee. Keep the card to use as a reference for your next meeting. (At this point, you have enough employee cards to buy a box for them.)

Mary felt Harry and others were taking advantage of her need to feel liked and to be fair. At the next meeting with Harry she made two major changes.

First, at the end of the meeting she and Harry recapped their discussion and she made notes and made him aware she was putting them in his file. Second, she made Harry responsible for reminding her of the next upcoming performance review and thus put the responsibility on him.

Epilogue

Truly inspiring your people means not just remembering but also following through on your promises and agreements.

47

Why There Is No Such Thing as "Fair" in Managing and Motivating People

One thing employers, parents, and politicians will hear again and again is that a decision they made wasn't fair to one person, or one group, or to one side of an argument. If you have been subjected to that criticism, there is hope for you.

Bob didn't realize his employees were playing him like a fiddle as they complained about his decisions about people, pay, and performance, and that the decisions weren't fair. He was in constant turmoil trying to rationalize and justify his decision-making. Finally, a convention speaker gave him the answer he needed. The speaker said, "Fair is always in the eye of the beholder, and every person will have a different definition of what is fair."

If you're going to try to be fair to every person in every situation, you'll never make any tough-minded decisions. There will always be someone screaming that you weren't fair or that the decision you made isn't fair, and you have to learn to tough it out and move on.

Assignment

On a 3 × 5 card, write down the following four points. Use them when you announce and explain any decision involving your people.

1. "I weighed all the facts and circumstances in this situation/issue/problem.

2. I discussed this situation/issue/problem with many of you before arriving at my decision.

3. I kept the interests of the organization and all of you in mind as I did so.

4. I made the best decision I could for all parties, and I'm not going to discuss it further.

Epilogue

When making tough decisions, consult everyone you think needs a voice. Use their input to help you make your decision. But once it's made—it's made.

48

3 Types of Motivation

Regardless of all you've read and heard about motivation, no topic is more confused than the misinformation and misunderstandings about motivation. Unfortunately, traditional motivation is external and uses a push to get people going. It assumes that people can be motivated by money or the things money buys, the consequences of failure (threats), or from inside, what we call inspiration.

As a consultant, I had many phone calls from owners and managers looking for a magic bullet to motivate their people. After discussion, we find their Excedrin headache is based on one of three things: Their people need training, their people need a different incentive plan, or their people just need a good dose of motivation. In almost every case, they are dead wrong. The problem is that they are listening to the symptoms of the problem and never really getting to the core issues at all, that they are lacking inspiration in what they are doing and in their organization.

Assignment

On a 3 × 5 card, write: "Motivation vs. Inspiration." As you continue to study this book and its ideas, begin to record some of the specific external actions you are taking that are traditional motivation. Then attempt to create an alternative set of tools that will inspire rather than motivate.

Epilogue

It is imperative that good leaders learn to inspire people and get them fired up from the inside out.

49

My Job Is to Sell You—YES, YOU CAN!

As a leader you must wear many different hats and fill many different job descriptions. Under your title of "inspirational leader" also hangs a subtitle that says "salesperson."

Motivational psychologists tell us that when we were born we only had two fears: the fear of falling and the fear of a loud noise. All other fears have been conditioned by our failures and by people telling us what we can't do. Psychologists call that *limiting beliefs*. If you want to inspire your people, become a CAN DO manager. Tell them that they are capable of doing things, not what they can't do.

Tell people what they can do and then encourage them to get it done and then brag about them when they do it. The more you encourage your people to stretch and break through those limiting beliefs that hold them back from fulfilling their individual capabilities, the more effective and productive they will become for you.

Assignment

On a 3 × 5 card, write out in large letters: "CAN DO." Post it where you can see it every morning to remind yourself that you are a CAN DO style of manager and leader.

Epilogue

As a CAN DO manager, don't give your people excuses why they might fail. When they bring those excuses to you, remind them of the limiting beliefs and encourage them to go for it.

50

Understanding the Role of Acceptance in Motivating Others

Do you know the people we most align ourselves with? Do you know who we see as an all-star performer? You are right. It is people who are most like us. We are most attracted to the people who are most like us and least attracted to the people who are our opposites. But learning to accept each person as an individual can result in a huge payoff to everyone trying to inspire others.

Upon being interviewed, one savvy sales manager who had won award after award for his talent with people said, "I know I'm a great sales manager because I know I am better than anyone who works for me, and I got over that a long time ago. I recognize different people have a different approach to getting a job successfully done. But that doesn't make it right or wrong." What a brilliant flash of the obvious.

Look at people's individuality and their strengths. The opposites may be exactly what you need. But when you can accept people for who they are and challenge them to compete with themselves only, you will make more progress in inspiring people than you ever dreamed possible.

> ### Assignment
>
> On a 3 × 5 card, write: "All people are different, and that is a strength, not a weakness. I appreciate that." Use this card to occasionally remind you of the truths about our differences.

Epilogue

As a wise professor said, "As people are, so shall they always be." You don't change the inner being of a person.

51

The 3 Things That Will Create Instant Team Synergy

Unless you can harness the team power of your people, you won't get results. No matter how much you transform your leadership style, how many programs you implement, how many new things you try, and no matter how much you want to accomplish, your big goals will elude you unless you can inspire your people to work together.

When Charlie bought the collection of 12 electrical parts distribution warehouses, he knew he had a tough road ahead. Two were marginally profitable, eight were about breaking even, and two were losing enough money that he seriously debated shuttering them. Instead, he decided to implement the three strategies that can bring a team together in a heartbeat.

Assignment

On a 5 × 7 card, write: "Common Enemy—Common Goals—Common Victories." Post this card by the exit of your office to remind you of this three-pronged method to building teamwork.

The first thing he focused on was to have a *common enemy*. In Charlie's case, he wisely chose to use internal issues, such as lost orders, delayed shipments, and paperwork errors. He challenged everyone to work as a team to make those problems go away.

His second team effort was to have *common goals*. He immediately adopted the idea of having 100 percent order-fill accuracy on every order, every day. He challenged his teams to achieve this goal, and within 60 days they reached a 98.5 percent accuracy rate—an enormous improvement. Having common goals and having everyone working toward that same end result had a huge payoff in Charlie's warehouses.

His third strategy was to celebrate *common victories*. His key goal was getting each and every warehouse location profitable. Charlie wisely bought a portable barbeque grill he could pull behind his car. And he made an agreement with each of his warehouses that by attacking their common enemy, and reaching their common goals, it would lead them to profitability. For any warehouse that achieved profitability, he would come and personally celebrate their victory by cooking lunch for them on his grill wearing his chef's hat. Within a year Charlie had all 12 warehouses in the profit zone, and a couple of them were making some really serious profits.

Epilogue

When you want to inspire a team or a group, take a look at the three things that can bring your group together in a heartbeat: a common enemy, common goals, and common victories.

52

Why Great Leaders Never Judge or Confront Their People

Many leaders claim to have an open door, but few have an open mind. As P. T. Barnum said, "Always tell me the truth, the whole truth, and nothing but the truth—even if it costs you your job." Resolving problems and concerns without people feeling attacked is a major challenge in inspiring people.

As a leader and a problem-solver, your job is to attack and resolve problems, not to attack people. There are no bad people, only poor, unacceptable, or bad behavior. The moment you move your focus from the problem to the person, people are likely to become resistant and defensive and feel as if their self-esteem is under assault, and they may fight back.

Assignment

On a 3 × 5 card, write: "Problems are behavior—not people." Often you will find it helpful to define what you're trying to accomplish in writing and leave people's names out of it. That way you can constantly refer back to it, as you have conversations and work on what you are trying to accomplish. Add this to your employee cards.

Epilogue
Very few people appreciate criticism, but most appreciate help in resolving the problems, issues, and challenges they have on a daily basis. Keep your focus on the behavior.

53

It's About Outcomes, Stupid!

You've probably had this happen to you at some point, and I'm sure it got under your skin. This belief that information is power is an old one from the old school of doing business from decades gone by. Yes, information is important. But real power comes from applying that information to get results. Action on the information is what creates the right outcomes for your company. My question is: How can your people get the right outcomes without having the necessary information? Answer: You can't!

> ### Assignment
>
> On a 3 × 5 card, write this reminder: "Tell my team everything I know as soon as I can. The more they know, the more effective and productive they will be." Put this in your tickler file to review once a week to remind yourself to keep you employees informed.

Jan Carlzon, famous for turning around SAS Airways some years back, said, "People who are given information cannot help but take responsibility for it, and people who are not given information cannot take responsibility for it." The issue for leaders these days is to keep their people fully informed so they can make intelligent decisions and help drive outcomes. It's about outcomes, stupid!

Epilogue

Inspiring people requires involving them in every hour of every day. You need to be on guard against the tendency to withhold information because it is power. People will perform better for you when they know what you know.

54

The 1 Deadly Error Managers Make When Delivering Criticism

If you have attempted to get your people to help you resolve problems or to take on tasks in your business and you haven't been successful, then you may be able to relate to this one fatal error that many managers make. If you've fumed, fussed, ranted, and raved but nothing worked, then you may well be guilty of trying to push people rather than pull them. You may be trying to order them to get involved instead of asking them to help.

Dale barked orders like an Army Sergeant running a basic training platoon. He would tell people what to do and try to push them into doing it, trying coercion. Unfortunately, when you push people, most push back. He failed to realize that what was really missing was asking for and getting their help in resolving problems and doing the things he wanted done.

There are two components in getting people beyond feeling that they are being forced to do things. First is to describe the problem, situation, or goal in a friendly manner. Don't make it intimidating by putting people down and criticizing. As Dale Carnegie said, any fool can criticize, condemn, or complain, and most of them do.

> ### Assignment
>
> On a 3 × 5 card, write this reminder: "When I want something done or I need help, ASK for it. Don't order it." Put it in your reminder file to review at least once each week.

Second, and most important, use the magic word: *help*. Ask for people to help you and you'll get further and quicker

81

action than trying to push them. William James, a noted motivational expert from Europe, said you have to have people with a "willing spirit." Dale Carnegie said, "Instill in them an eager want and they will help you."

Epilogue

When people are asked to help and they feel that their assistance is valued, they are far more likely to be on your team than when they feel that they're being forced to participate.

55

CP1 = EN1

About 50 years ago, give or take a decade, American business began a change downhill that continues today. We have labeled this change "dehumanizing." We've taken the emotion out of business, and people are acting as robots. Businesses want to use high-tech, low-touch, or no-touch. They want to have as little interaction with the customer and get as much money as they can. How often do you feel as though you're treated as a number by people with all of the enthusiasm and excitement of watching paint dry? Unfortunately, too many managers take this approach with their employees, too.

A Texas marketing class teaches a principle that says people will go where they get their emotional needs met. We've added what we call CP1, which is core principle number one, equals EN1. EN1 means emotional needs first.

When you have an interaction with an employee on the phone, in person, or in any other context, remember to deal with his or her emotional needs before you get to material needs and business needs. You might remember it in this way: By using the acronym WARN, we are warning you that you need to meet their human needs. W-A-R-N stands for people wanting to be wanted, appreciated, respected, and needed. And the business that provides that and those old-fashioned good feelings in today's high-tech world will have high-quality employees beating a path through its door. Why shouldn't that be you?

Assignment

On a 3 × 5 card, write "CP1 = EN1." Under it write "Core Principle One = Emotional Needs One." Then write: "WARN: Wanted, Appreciated, Respected, Needed." File this card to review once a week to remind you of your employees emotional needs.

Epilogue

Walt Disney said, "Create a place where children want to go, and their parents will follow." Why do children flock to Disney and drag their parents along? Because they get their emotional needs met.

56

Celebrate: Turn Little Times Into Big Ones

Have you ever heard someone complain about getting too much praise, recognition, or positive feedback? I doubt it. Most of us both need and want to feel appreciated in the work we do. Survey after survey has shown that one failure of managers, supervisors, and leaders was not giving enough positive feedback.

Big Al, as he was known, ran a series of warehouses and was both highly successful and well respected as a businessperson. At a meeting he was talking about his secrets of inspiring people and he shared one nugget that has proven to be a powerful tool for inspiring people. His wisdom was to make big times out of little ones. You don't always have to achieve major successes to praise an employee.

Employees respond best, are energized best, to do their best work when they are recognized for the good things they do—even the small things.

Assignment

On a 3 × 5 card, write: "Praise—Performance." Review this card from your tickler file once a week to remind yourself to provide positive feedback routinely.

Epilogue

Recognize and celebrate each success by every employee, no matter how small. A simple word of praise or congratulation is usually all that's needed.

57

1 Word to Master: Leadership

There is an old saying that managers do things right and leaders do the right things. This often leaves management in a quandary. You need results, and your income depends on the performance of your people, but you're not sure if you want to be at their mercy. It's no fun to be a leader to work with a bunch of whiny, spoiled, lazy employees. If anyone tells you that if you love your people, everything will be fine, you can be assured it won't. They need you to lead. They need you to create a powerful vision; harness their strengths; inspire their spirits; and take them into the market with fire, zest, and awesome enthusiasm.

Colin Powell said leadership is the art of accomplishing more than the science of management says is possible. No one likes to work in an environment where there are no rules and anything goes. Your people need and want structure, and they will respect you for providing it. If in the past you've called yourself a manager, a boss, a supervisor, or any similar terms, today is the day to change that terminology and call yourself a leader. See yourself out in front of a group; picture yourself with a marching band as the bandleader.

> ### *Assignment*
> On a 3 × 5 card write the following: "Lead, follow, or get the hell out of the way." Post it prominently in your office or workspace. Let it remind you that you should be a leader.

> ### Epilogue
> *People need leadership. Without it, people become demoralized and incapacitated; some become permanently turned off and lose all future potential.*

58

Courage vs. Conformity

As a leader, your role is to create sanity in a chaotic world without destroying the creative, flexible culture your people need. That's what we're all seeking as leaders: how to walk the fine line between chaos, creativity, and sanity. As a leader, it's your job to figure out a way to win again and again in a permanently changing world.

> ### Assignment
>
> On a 3 × 5 card, write: "Have the courage to lead with new ideas and win." Review it once a week to remind yourself that you are a leader and responsible for creating new ideas for success and leading your team in that direction.

When Stanley Galt was hired as the CEO of Goodyear Tire & Rubber Company, the company was losing money. The red ink was flowing. Stanley immediately had the courage to get everyone at Goodyear focused on selling tires. They went out into the marketplace to hunt down anybody and everybody who might possibly sell Goodyear tires. As CEO of Goodyear, Stanley developed the habit of spending every Saturday morning in a tire dealer's store to keep abreast of what they needed and wanted from tire manufacturers. He had the courage to break the rules, take on clients that others said they shouldn't, and stand his ground. Within one year Stanley had used his courage to break the rules and do things differently, and he had Goodyear in the black. He had the courage to sell himself out of a black hole by leading with new ideas.

> **Epilogue**
> *When you find the courage to do things differently and break away from conformity, think about using the words* improvement *and* transition, *and other types of words that don't mean something will be brand new.*

59

To Be Effective, Do More Than "Walk the Talk"

As a leader, your goal should be to create a shared vision of values and integrity, ultimately leading to a great reputation of living your life as a model for the way the company lives its life. You succeed by helping others succeed. Their success is your success, and if they don't succeed, it's unlikely that you will either.

When Mike, the CEO of a respected Chicago manufacturing company, learned that his sales manager had made an error in calculating a promotion bonus promised to a customer, he asked how much it would cost him to follow through on their promise. The customer was expecting several thousand dollars that it really didn't deserve as a part of the promotion. In an effort to protect their reputation, Mike told the sales manager to follow through and pay the customer, because they had made the promise and set the expectation. He was demonstrating, living, and doing more than just talking their values. And everyone was watching: his sales manager, the customer, and his competitors. Even though he would not recover that much

> **Assignment**
>
> On a 3 × 5 card, write: "Lead by walking the talk." Use this card to remind you that you set the standard for your team's values and standards, and you set more by your behaviors than by your speech.

money from that customer in years to come, he knew overall it would come back to him in his reputation.

Leading by example is demonstrated, not just talked. It is talking, living, and protecting the virtues you deem important to your success and to the success of your company.

Epilogue

Long-term success tends to be reserved for people of character whose leadership style fits their talk.

60

Meeting Their Needs: Create a Salad Bar

Today, more than ever, employees want more than a one-size-fits-all approach to options and choices for pay and benefits. Desirable employees want the flexibility to customize their compensation plans with employers. They know they can get a job elsewhere that offers such agreements, and so you need to offer it also.

When a sales organization announced that the top three salespeople could win a deluxe round trip to Hawaii in the next sales contest, one of the salespeople went home and shared that news with his wife. She was devastated. She explained that they needed money for braces for the kids, the car needed repairs, and some things around the house needed to be fixed. Rather than go to Hawaii, she would rather have had the cash. As a result of offering this promotion with no flexibility, this company lost its very best salesman when he went to a company that would let him pick the prize he might win.

It's imperative that you know the rules and regulations regarding pay and benefits. Today there are many new options, and you need to know, use, and offer them to your employees in a salad-bar approach if you're going to truly inspire and retain the people you want.

Assignment

On a 3 × 5 card, write: "Be flexible in pay, benefits, and incentives." Review the card before salary reviews and benefits reviews, and before you set up incentive programs. Make them flexible so you can retain the best.

Epilogue

Today, employees want to feel in control, and the one thing a salad-bar approach does is give them that feeling and benefit.

61

Positive Models:
Your Way or the Highway

When it comes to inspiring people, their involvement and input are essential if you are going to get them to buy into your plans. However, after the mold is cast and the plans are made, it is essential that everyone follow your plans and guidelines to present a clear and consistent impression of your company to customers again and again and again.

When Larry proudly showed up for work on his Harley Davidson, he also was wearing the full Harley "uniform": black leather chaps and all the accessories that go with it. After his boss ooh-ed and aah-ed about his new Harley and congratulated him on all the work he had done to earn the money, he then asked Larry if he realized he didn't have a lot of time to go home and change clothes and come back in the company uniform. Larry commented, "You mean I can't wear my Harley gear at work today?" And his boss said, friendly but firm, "No, I'm sorry. We all wear a company uniform, and there are no exceptions." Larry went home and changed.

> ### Assignment
>
> On a 3 × 5 card, write: "Be friendly but firm on company standards and expectations." It should remind you as you occasionally review this card that you need to set the standards and expectations, then enforce them in a friendly but firm manner.

You need to be friendly but firm and be a demanding boss if you are going to make sure the impressions you give are consistent. You can't let everybody have a voice in the day-to-day appearance of your company, your logo, colors, uniforms, and so on.

Epilogue

Remember, in carrying out your plan, that you are not running a democracy. You're running a benevolent dictatorship.

62

Your Speed = Their Speed

In the old economy of years gone by, leadership was about encouraging your people to thrive, no matter what the circumstances. Leadership today is about giving your people what they need so they can support the speed and intensity that the work demands from them. You need to realize that, as the leader, you are both the gas and the brakes for your organization. The speed of leader will be the speed of the team.

For many years I lived in Indianapolis, the home of the famous Indy 500 race. Each year, excitement abounds as the pace car circles the track followed by those high-speed, incredibly fast racing machines waiting to go around that track at breakneck speeds. But the catch is that when the pace car's on the track, no one is allowed to go faster than the pace car without being penalized. We've invented computers, cell phones, Palm Pilots, text messaging, and, of course, the Internet. Business is moving at a torrid pace. You need to realize that your organization will be no faster or any slower

Assignment

On a 3 × 5 card for weekly review, write: "I set the standards for how fast or slowly we get things done by how I behave and get my own work done." This should remind you that your team will gauge their own speed on your speed.

than the leadership you give it. If you do only one thing to inspire your team in the days ahead, create a sense of urgency about getting things done. By your own behaviors and intensity, set the speed as an example for them.

Epilogue

Be sure to consistently ask your staff if they need to go faster and how you can help them get there, as their leader.

63

What Is Your Role in Inspiring People in a World of Negative Messages?

For reasons no one can fully explain, we are bombarded 24/7 with negative news filled with tragedy, gloom, and doubt. Every aspect of the media, from newspapers to TV to radio, seems to perpetuate bad news. Don't let yourself and your organization be dragged down and demoralized by these purveyors of doom.

Noted author William James said, "As a man thinketh so is he." Everyone needs a pick-me-up bouquet to counterbalance the challenges and the negative messages they hear each day. Develop the habit of being a light in a dark world. Make it your job assignment to point out the positives that your people accomplish and what can be accomplished when everyone works together. Remember: 5 percent unemployment means that 95 percent are still working, have money to spend, and need products and services.

Assignment

On a 3 × 5 card, record the following: "I set the emotional environment in my workplace by the positive and upbeat attitude I display." This will remind you upon your weekly review that you are the person who your team members look to to counterbalance the negative in their lives and create an upbeat environment in which for them to work.

Epilogue

As the old saying goes, "If you think you can, you can, and if you think you can't, you can't." Your role is to be a can-do inspirer of people.

64

Don't Be a Know-It-All

As leaders, we are often wrong if we believe that our people expect us to know everything that is going on and to have all the answers. In reality, no leader in today's complex business world can have all the answers or be up to speed in every subject area. The single most important question you can add to your vocabulary is this: "What do you think?" We need to be mental midgets and to ask other people their opinions.

> ### *Assignment*
>
> On one of your weekly review 3 × 5 cards, write: "What do you think? Asking for opinions and information makes me more informed, more aware of what is going on, more inclusive in my style, and more effective in my leadership."

While doing a consulting project for a COO named Ed, it became quickly obvious he ran his organization by fear and intimidation. People were afraid to speak out. When I commented to another senior consultant that he was the first executive I had ever met who knew how to do everybody's job better than they did, my friend looked at me and said, "Yes, he knows how to do everyone else's job except his own." He would have been far better off not being a know-it-all.

People are both flattered and inspired when you ask their opinions. Don't be afraid as a leader to admit that you need the input from others. Their opinions are critically important in providing you information you need to be an effective leader.

Epilogue

*The real ideas, the real answers, and the real inspiration you
need are spread out among your workers.*

65

Shoveling Coal and 4 Crucial Questions

Today, more than ever, workers want to be involved in what
is going on and to know how they are doing. They want to
know if they are moving forward, falling back, or just standing
in place.

One division manager told me that he often feels so left out
that it's as if he's down in a dingy, dark boiler room shoveling
coal. The company wants him to shovel more and more coal
and to keep the boilers going, but they rarely let him come up
and find out what is going on. It is even more unusual when
someone from leadership comes down to the boiler room from
"mahogany row" and talks to him.

There are four key questions that every employee wants
answered and would like to know on a daily basis:

1. How am I doing?
2. Where am I going?
3. What am I part of?
4. What will it mean for me when we succeed?

95

Your role is to make sure those four questions are answered again and again and again. And, the worst part is to assume that your people know. Don't wait for them to ask.

Assignment

On a 3 × 5 card for weekly review, write the four questions identified on page 95. Let this card remind you that these are the four key pieces of information your team members want regularly. Provide it.

Epilogue

Are you putting people into a hole or leaving them in a vacuum by not communicating with them? Remember that they will see this as harsh punishment instead of just missing communication.

66

Your Culture Is NOT a Democracy

One of the crucial lessons every leader must grasp is that successful leaders mold, shape, and create their company culture rather than let it just happen. They proactively decide the vision, values, and principles that the company will live by and then jealously protect and direct that culture on a daily basis. Are you letting your company culture guide you, or are you guiding your company culture?

When Ralph's company was near bankruptcy, the consultant he called in quickly found that the company lacked direction and had totally abandoned the culture, values, and principles that had made it successful in earlier years. Ralph's first and most important function was to resurrect the old thinking that had guided the company so successfully. The workforce applauded his efforts, and over the months that followed the company was rescued from the date with the grim reaper. He made sure that they were using the company culture in a proactive manner. He led the way.

Your company culture will ultimately shape and color your company attitudes, your company service philosophies, and the reputation that you earn with customers. Leaders demonstrate this by their behaviors and by their insistence on it from their employees.

Assignment

Remember that 3 × 5 cards that says: "Lead, follow, or get out of the way"? It works here, too.

Epilogue

Study the stories of many successful leaders, from Jack Welsh at General Electric to Walt Disney at Disney & Company to Ray Kroc, the founder of McDonalds, and you will find the one commonality is that they took control of their companies cultures.

67

Rules vs. Guidelines: Know the Difference

Are your people inspired and empowered to use both their brawn and their brains in doing their job each day? If your approach to management is operating with manual after manual of rules and regulations, you are surely suffocating your people and causing them to lose their ability to be creative and grow.

When Dale took over a highly successful retail store that had been in the same location for more than 20 years, his first management action was to tighten up and make rules and regulations for virtually everything his people had to do. It was totally inflexible. Very soon his employees felt like robots or prisoners in handcuffs and shackles; they weren't allowed to make any decisions. His rules caused all decisions to go to Dale, and simply getting to him became a real nightmare, as he was so busy putting out fires and trying to run the entire ship by himself. Very soon his good employees began to leave—and so did his customers.

Whenever possible, rethink what you call Rules and Regulations and instead issue guidelines for your people to follow. Tell them that they are intelligent, they know what they're doing, and you know they are going to make good decisions. Empower them to truly be creative in working with customers within general guidelines, not rigid rules.

> **Assignment**
>
> On a 3 × 5 card write: "Review and revise our rules into guidelines that empower the team, not restrict the team." Then do it. Set a goal of reviewing your policies and procedures to empower your team to be successful, not limit them.

> **Epilogue**
>
> *There are too many variables and too many different situations for your people to have rules and regulations for everything they do.*

68

You Can't Be Fired Unless...

All employees realize that their employer has the ultimate power over them: the ability to fire them—with or without a cause or reason. If you are drop-dead serious about inspiring your people, then management by intimidation and using the word *firing* will rarely be part of your conversation with your team. In fact, you will see firing as an undesirable last resort only.

When Ruth Ann was called to her supervisor's office, she thought they were going to be discussing the project she was working on. She thought her performance was good and had gotten compliments in the days gone by. Little did she realize she

Assignment

There are certain absolutes on any job that should result in firing. On a 3 × 5 card, write down each of these actions or events (such as theft, lying to you or a customer, drinking on the job, or failing to come to work). There are others. Communicate these to all your employees so it is clear to them what the absolute firing behaviors are. Then, remember to remind people of these at the same time you remind then of your performance standards and expectations.

was about to be fired, without a clear explanation. In fact, her supervisor had really never been one to communicate very openly, and Ruth Ann was always left guessing about what was expected of her in carrying out her duties. The firing devastated her.

It was sad that her boss didn't tell or teach her what to do and then fired her for not having done it. The problem with firing and using intimidation in management is that it not only demoralizes the person dismissed, but it has a negative impact on your entire workforce. People begin to doubt you and doubt the organization for which they work.

Epilogue
By making it clear why people can be fired they also know under what grounds they cannot be fired.

69

Kill the Snake!

A grave danger when dealing with mistakes, rule violations, and employees who don't play by the book is to use that event to punish and suffocate everyone because of one person's missteps or an isolated incident. Overreacting and using mass punishment (remember grade school?) can stifle your people and destroy the inspiration you're working hard to create.

When past presidential candidate H. Ross Perot sold his company to General Motors, he said he was amazed at how General Motors handled problems and situations. He related it to discovering a snake in your path. He said that at General

Motors, when they discovered a snake, the first thing they did is hire a consultant to study snakes. They formed a committee to talk about snakes. Their management went out looking for snakes. Then they would start out rooting out snakes by killing anything that even looked like a snake or was near a snake.

On the other hand, Perot's style was this: When you see a snake, you simply get a hoe and cut off its head. The lesson here is to beware of making rules and regulations for isolated incidents that impact everyone, and don't use mass punishment for a single person's actions. Ask yourself if it is really something that needs to have broad regulations or if it is one incident where you cut off its head and move on.

Assignment

On a 3 × 5 card, write: "Just kill the snake; don't regulate it away or wipe out everyone near it." Review this card occasionally, especially when you have a problem you need to deal with, so it will remind you to just take care of the snake without mass punishment and without massive new regulations to make certain there are no more snakes.

Epilogue

The more freedom you can give your people and the less rules and regulations you need in the workplace, the better off you are.

70

America's Promise: Equal Rights

Today it seems that many, many people are yelling, shouting, and demanding equal rights. They want to be protected. They want someone to put everybody on a level playing field. It is important to recognize that our ancestors came to America with one important idea in mind: They wanted *the equal right to be unequal*. They wanted to be judged for their performance and have the opportunity to excel in America. Thus, we have today's meritocracy—where people are judged by their accomplishments.

> ### Assignment
>
> On a 3 × 5 card, write: "Everyone has the equal right to excel. Those who do will be rewarded." Consider posting this around the workspace to remind your employees that outcomes count.

Jack was a manager who was always trying to make sure everybody who worked for him was happy. He tried to balance everything and failed to see that he should really be judging people by their behavior and their outcomes. He finally got a wake-up call when he began to lose good people who were not recognized for what they had accomplished. Jack learned, as you must also, to only judge people by their attitudes, their productivity, and their accomplishments.

When we succumb to the idea of everyone being equal, then we stifle people's opportunities to excel. We diminish a person's inspiration and throw water on the fire instead of encouraging himor her to be the best he or she can be as an individual. That's what has made America great: the equal right to be unequal.

Epilogue

Not all employees are equal. Make an extra effort to recognize and reward those people who produce the most for you.

71

ASK—It Is Easier to Stay Out of Trouble

How many times have you found yourself getting pulled into a situation that at first seems simple and clear cut, only to find that circumstances escalated and it evolved into a nightmare? Issues such as employee firings and customer threats come to mind most often.

As an attorney, my friend Tom provided his business clients one of the most valuable services any attorney could ever offer: again and again he reminded me and others that it is easier to *stay* out of trouble than to *get* out of trouble.

Assignment

The quality and quantity of your Rolodex of advisors are critical. Have these people and their phone numbers handy. Make a 3 × 5 card with their names and numbers listed and put it in the front of your set of 3 × 5 cards for quick reference. If you discover that you are missing someone important, develop a new consultant. At a minimum, you should have an attorney, accountant, HR expert, and management expert available. Certainly, depending on your industry, you might want others.

His message was that when you even smell a hint of trouble, it's time to pick up the phone and call your attorney, CPA, or other consulting advisors and get advice before the problem becomes one that overpowers you. Don't wait until you've stepped into quicksand to look for a rope.

Epilogue

It is better to have a list of advisors and consultants and not need them, than to need them and not have them.

72

Are You a Conformist?

Have you ever asked yourself why you do things the way you do? Let me suggest there are two reasons. First, it's the way you were taught, because that's the way everybody else has done it, and, second, you've always done it that way so why would you change. Perhaps we need to adopt a new philosophy: "If it ain't broke, break it."

One conference speaker said people who are afraid to challenge their own beliefs are timid feeders in the lagoon. Dr. Robert Shuler, legendary motivational expert, asked the question, "What would you attempt to do if you absolutely, positively knew you could not fail?" If there's no chance for it to go wrong, which of your ideas would you try to implement?

Think about the great inventions, cures, and creativity we've seen through the years. People who tried, experimented, and were always looking for a better way are those who have changed our world. Are you looking for a more efficient way or a better outcome?

Assignment

Brainstorm some ideas you would like to try: new procedures, new concepts, new policies, new approaches. Now list at least five of these on a 3 × 5 card. Over a period of several months, try out one idea at a time. Yes, some will fail, but some will also succeed. And you will be making a huge difference. This, too, is part of leadership. Your team will respect you all the more for innovation

Epilogue

Dr. Shuler is also known for having said that he would rather attempt to do something great and fail than attempt to do nothing and succeed.

73

Sell Your Unique Strengths—No Layoffs

If you have a track record of steady employment and no layoffs, that can be a powerful tool for hiring, retaining, and inspiring people. We call it harnessing and using your SBA (small business advantage). David was small but had an advantage over Goliath. Use your tools in the same way.

Assignment

On a 3 × 5 card, list all of your small business advantages, such as the ability to make quick decisions, owner's availability and accessibility in the company, and so on. Then use this card when you are hiring new people and use it to remind current employees they are working for a good company.

One employer had a tough time hiring entry-level people because he couldn't justify paying them the hourly wage that many of their friends and colleagues earned in other jobs. At the same time he knew that a big advantage of working for him was that they would get 52 paychecks with no layoffs, whereas many of their friends were collecting food stamps and unemployment because their employment wasn't steady. He turned his no layoffs into a commercial, both in his hiring and as a reminder for his current employees.

Epilogue

Tell your people that it's your intention that they never be laid off and that if they help you and work with you, that's almost a certainty.

74

Monkey See, Monkey Do

In recent years, researchers have made tremendous progress in understanding how animals teach their young. The rule of the animal kingdom follows the old saying "monkey see, monkey do." Almost all training by animals is by observation. Their youngsters learn by working with and watching Mom and Dad, and people learn much the same way.

Recently, my local library underwent a multi-million-dollar renovation, and it is fabulous. As you enter the library, there is a large sign that says, "No food or beverages allowed." On a recent visit, the lady who works at the information desk in the center of the library came walking across the lobby with a large cup of soda. A maintenance man walked by with a bag of chips in his hand. Now, what are we supposed to believe? The sign, or what we see? Monkey see, monkey do.

Assignment

On an 3 × 5 card write: "Monkey see, monkey do" and post it somewhere in your office as a reminder that you are the primary behavioral role model for your employees. They will do as you do. If you do it right, so will they.

Remember that almost all of what your people will model will come from *your* behavior. What they see you do is what they will do on the job. The great confusion comes when you tell them to do one thing, and they see you doing something different. You are a role model for your team, and you've got to walk the talk, and talk the walk.

> **Epilogue**
> *Your people want and need a good role model. Remember: they are watching you!*

75

Read Your Job Description

One way to prove you are a red-blooded, normal human being is to admit you've procrastinated on confronting tough workforce issues such as discipline, arguments, personality clashes, and especially having to let someone go. These are always a real dilemma for anyone dealing with human resources. The problem is that decisions are not clear cut, and personalities always enter into those situations.

> **Assignment**
>
> On a 3 × 5 card write: "Don't procrastinate on personnel issues. Like rotten meat, they only smell worse with time." Use this card to remind yourself that these issues must be dealt with—and that's your job, not someone else's.

One of the challenges doctors face is getting people to take their medicine. They take part of the prescription, are feeling better, and move on. But in reality, they need to take it all to make sure they've dealt totally and completely with their problems. The same is true with managers. Sometimes we just don't want to take our medicine. A simple way to get yourself inspired to face the tough issues is to read your job description. You and you alone are responsible for making sure that these issues are dealt with—

not just effectively, but also in a timely manner. *Bad news does not get better with age.*

Epilogue

Success builds success. The time you spend procrastinating and worrying about a situation could be used to inspire people instead of rehashing what you might do over and over again.

76

Intentions Are as Important as Actions

In public relations training, one key principle is to be very careful publicizing what you intend to do and instead to use a megaphone to shout and tout your accomplishments. In other words, play down your to-do list and play up your to-done list.

Sears Roebuck was one of the first major retailers to adopt today's overused message of total customer satisfaction guaranteed. Sears earned a deep trust with customers by declaring its intentions of total customer satisfaction and then following through. Sears became legendary by selling its Craftsman tool line to both professionals and amateurs, who opted for Sears tools knowing that Sears intended

Assignment

It is critical that you follow through with your statements and your promises, especially to employees. On a 3 × 5 card to be reviewed weekly, write: "Intentions are great; deeds are better." Use the card to remind you that you absolutely must follow through on your intentions, stated or otherwise.

to replace or refund them if they failed for any reason in their lifetime.

Lesson learned: Intentions may be more valued than your actions, but only if you live up to the words you say. In other words, your follow-through will be the final determination if people believe your intentions.

Epilogue

Employees and customers alike will value your intentions when you prove them by following through and reporting on your accomplishments.

77

The 1 Thing You Must Do to Get Employees to Respect You

Assignment

"Consistency leads to predictability and to respect." Write that on a 3 × 5 card to remind you to be consistent in your activities and your decisions regarding employees. This will lead to respect. Review this card periodically.

To be a truly effective and inspirational leader, the "ideal" would be that people both like you and respect you. Because liking you is largely a popularity decision, the one absolute in your leadership equation is that your people *must* respect you. Without their respect your leadership will flounder like a ship without a rudder.

In study after study, when employees were asked the single most important value a leader needed to gain their respect, the same answer surfaced again and again: your people want you to *be consistent* even when they may disagree with your choices and decision-making.

Why is consistency such a must to your leadership? Consistency equals predictability and is the key ingredient to earning their trust over time.

Epilogue

Although being liked is desirable for all leaders, respect is even more important.

78

The Man in the Mirror

Experts agree that the one most important relationship you will struggle with in your life is the one you have with your inner self. Accept the fact that you will never please all of the people all of the time and turn your attention to satisfying the person you see in the mirror each and every day.

When a friend finally realized her spouse had no interest in salvaging their troubled marriage, she was overwhelmed with well-meaning friends and family advising her to get even with him, to make him pay, and to

Assignment

One test of any decision is to look in the mirror and ask the person you see there if he or she agrees. On a 3 × 5 card, write: "Ask the man in the mirror when in doubt." Rely on his or her answer. Review the card occasionally to remind you of this test.

punish him for failing to live up to their wedding vows. Though she listened to more advice than she really wanted, my friend decided to take the high road in their divorce proceedings. She decided to end the marriage with class, dignity, and the goal of remaining on good terms with her ex.

She decided the one person she had to live with most of all was herself. She decided to listen to the person in the mirror. Have you done that?

Epilogue

Remind yourself that the one person you can't escape from is you. Value the person in the mirror.

79

The H.E.L.M. Principle

All leaders need a set of standards by which they can test and weigh many of the tough choices and ethical decisions they must make. All too often, rather than being black and white, these choices are shades of gray, clouding the decision-making process.

George has earned the deep respect of his reps and customers nationwide in his role as national sales manager for a variety of respected companies. This respect is rooted in his uncanny sense of right and wrong and his track record of doing the right thing in some murky and difficult situations. Early on, George found a filter system for guiding his decision process. He labeled it the "H.E.L.M. Principle." When faced with making ethical decisions, George asked himself these questions: Is

Assignment

On a 3 × 5 card, write out the H.E.L.M. Principle:

"Is my decision:

Honest?

Ethical?

Legal?

Moral?"

Review the card every time you need to make a tough decision to help guide you to the best answer.

my choice honest, is my choice ethical, is my choice legal, and is it moral?

If the answer is a resounding yes, he is good to go, and if the choice screams and shouts "don't do it," he doesn't—a good set of guiding principles that you can adapt.

Epilogue

Decisions involving people are the most difficult you have to make. Make the best decisions you can, and make them timely. Use the H.E.L.M. Principle to help.

80

Integrity: When 2 People Know

There's an old adage that the only way two people can keep a secret is that if one of them is dead. The very moment you leak sensitive information or share a secret with another person, it is almost guaranteed your secret will soon become public knowledge. As the World War II saying goes, "loose lips sink ships."

When law enforcement officers read suspects their rights, they always tell the person he or she has the right to remain silent. The problem is that most people don't have the will to keep their mouths shut.

When dealing with competitive issues, personnel concerns, or sensitive changes in your business, learn to remain silent. Leaks and gossip can be deadly in terms of eating away at trust, loyalty, and inspiration. If you keep mum, your secrets are safe and secure.

Assignment

"Loose lips sink ships." Write that on a 3 × 5 card and review it routinely. Keep sensitive information to yourself.

Epilogue

Sometimes you need to keep information to yourself to protect it from the competition—not from your employees.

81

Mom, Sunday School, and a Grand Jury

You already know how fragile your company reputation is, having witnessed other businesses being bruised, battered, and even crushed by negative publicity in the public eye. Keeping your people inspired and on target demands constantly searching for innovative ways to protect your venerable reputation.

Bill, an engineer, found an interesting way to have his people test the things they bragged about in describing their work. His litmus test: Could you brag about what you're doing to your mother, would you feel free to teach

> ### Assignment
> Write down this litmus test on one of your 3 × 5 cards: "Can I brag about what I'm doing to my mother, teach it to my Sunday school class, or present it to a grand jury?" Occasionally, when you are discussing completed actions with employees, ask them to apply it to a recent situation they've handled or encountered.

it to your Sunday school class, and could it stand the scrutiny and interrogation of a grand jury? Such testing is intended to give your workforce a frame of reference about how their behavior and actions could be viewed by outsiders. They can use it to be a green light for go, a yellow light for caution, or a red light for stop. They can catch inappropriate actions before they get legs.

> ### Epilogue
> *Protecting the perception others have of you and your company or organization means involving everyone to be vigilant and on guard to inappropriate public scrutiny.*

82

Faith, Failure, and Forgiveness

Of all the burdens you will ever carry, the heaviest one is carrying a grudge. Becoming an inspirational leader means facing our fatal human flaws. Two of those human traits are the failure to recognize and admit that we make mistakes, and the struggle we face in letting go of our feelings of failure and guilt.

> ### Assignment
> When weighing mistakes, can you encourage everyone to stop, admit their mistakes, and ask themselves, "What lesson did I learn from this, and why can't I forgive myself and move on?" Write this statement on a 3 × 5 card for occasional review.

Dale was known as a hothead and, though he was an astute business owner, his sudden explosions of anger often alienated his workers. Such outbursts were so destructive that Dale's business ultimately failed. Of course, he blamed everyone except himself. Dale fell into the same trap common to all too many people, looking everywhere but inside for the answers to his bitterness, anger, and resentment.

Learning to forgive, forget, and move on is one of the most valuable qualities any leader can develop, and learning to forgive ourselves should be our first effort. After all, we pay the price for the burdens we bear, and those at whom we're angry may not even know about how those concerns are eating away at us.

> ### Epilogue
> *When you talk to yourself, be reminded that mistakes are human and the key is to learn from them.*

83

Inside and Outside Listening Mechanisms

Nothing is more valuable, inspires trust, and motivates employees than to hear other people sing praises about you and your company. At the same time, everyone must be taught and constantly reminded how negative talk can have a wrecking-ball effect to tear down your reputation. It can take years to build a positive image, and it can come tumbling down with one inappropriate situation or comment.

Imagine how the customers who were waiting for service probably interpreted some off-handed comments by employees in a packing and shipping store. As a customer was inquiring about guaranteed overnight delivery of his laptop to the West Coast, this employee became a loose cannon, telling his customer that the cost his company charged for such service was totally outrageous and he would be a fool to pay it; he should package and ship it himself. The customer quietly said he wasn't greatly concerned about the cost and just wanted to know

Assignment

You might adopt this creed: If you can't say something good about your company, don't say anything at all. Every employee should be trained to be a listening post, both inside and outside the company, to alert management when they hear inappropriate remarks about the company. To remember this key point, create a 3 × 5 card with the following: "Loose lips sink ships. Everyone should talk positively about the company. Come to me if you can't and we'll work it out." Use the card to remind team members of this occasionally.

if the young man could get the job done and guarantee its delivery. When he said yes, he went about the purchase and went out the door. One always has to wonder how much damage was done by one employee and his poor perception of why his company charges what it does for the services it offers.

Epilogue

Everyone needs to be reminded to put up red flags when they hear even flippant, off-hand negative comments about the company.

84

Work ON, Not IN Your Business

One of the interesting phenomena about humans is how we enjoy getting caught up in the activity trap. It is so easy for the business to be running us instead of us running the business. As a consultant, I've watched people repeatedly get caught up in majoring in minors: getting sidetracked by the majority and failing to manage the critical few. It can be a terminal illness.

Jack, the son of an entrepreneur/owner, became the CEO of his company when his father retired, and he was always too busy, caught up in activities, to be developing new customers and inspiring new people. When the tragic news came that the company had lost its biggest customer—a customer that represented more than 60 percent of its business—Jack was faced with one of two choices: either he had to either make time to inspire people

118

and oversee their marketing; or lay off many of his valuable, seasoned, and enthusiastic workers. Suddenly Jack realized that he had to take control of his time and *make time* to work ON his business, not just work IN his business.

The single greatest advice that any consultant can give you, or that your mother might tell you, is that you must make time to work on your business. Get away, make time to sit down with a cup of coffee or soda, and outline your challenges. Think about what needs to be done. Make time for yourself to make those improvements.

Assignment

"Make time to work ON your business, not just IN your business." Write that on a 3 × 5 care and review weekly to remind yourself of how you must take control of your time to control your business.

Epilogue
You must assign time blocks and proactively control what you want to get done if you are going to work on your business, not just in your business.

85

Boss, Heal Thyself— For You Are the Problem

Why is it that the boss never has time to even think about getting caught up, whereas some subordinates never seem to have enough to do? If this age-old paradox has plagued you, there is hope. Perhaps you need a "checkup from the neck up" to identify the source of this workload imbalance. Maybe the problem is closer to home than you realize.

When Sandy announced to her boss that she was caught up and had absolutely nothing to do, she could tell he was both stunned and shocked by her announcement. His silence must have telegraphed a warning to her. Fortunately, he responded by requesting some time to think over her comments and told her he would get back to her shortly. She retreated in fear that her announcement may have provoked him to attack her or even fire her for admitting she had nothing to do.

Fortunately, Sandy's boss pondered how a sales rep with 350 customers and 600 prospects could possibly have nothing to do. With 600 prospects not yet customers, she could not possibly be "caught up." Then he found the problem: it was him. He had not made her job description clear, and he had failed miserably to make sure she had appropriate goals and objectives and a "can do" action plan. He knew that not making it clear as to what her real job was made it time to fire the boss.

Assignment

We're back to the boss and setting expectations for the team members. Sometimes it requires the leader to lead by reviewing the guidance provided to employees to make certain it is appropriate. On a 3 × 5 card, write the following for occasional review: "If someone is 'caught up' with his or her work, either he or she has too little work or too little guidance. Both are my fault, not theirs."

Epilogue

When you see people that appear not to have enough to do, the first place to look is the last place most people do. Maybe it's time to fire yourself.

86

It Won't Get Better With Age

It has been said that life is about "managing a series of ongoing challenges interrupted by a periodic crisis." If there's one area where improvement can inspire yourself and others, it is developing the discipline to tackle and resolve these never-ending challenges with a decisive, can-do attitude.

The idea that the best time to eat a frog is first thing in the morning may be a bit graphic for you, but the discipline of getting unpleasant tasks out of the way quickly and decisively can be an inspiration for everyone involved. When avoidance, delay, and procrastination are present, they rarely resolve any dilemma. As things hang on, they linger and fester, and they rob you and everyone around you of the enthusiasm, inspiration, and motivation you need to tackle your positive business opportunities. Delaying the tackling of tough assignments is an incredibly debilitating de-motivator that eats away at the inspiration of your workforce.

> ### Assignment
> On a 3 × 5 card, write: "Eat the frog early." This should remind you of the principle of dealing with the unpleasant quickly and early so you can get on with the good stuff.

> ### Epilogue
> *The relief that comes from getting unpleasant situations out of the way and moving on to more desirable things can have a huge payoff.*

87

Facelift, Extreme Makeover—Good Getting Better

You don't have to be terminally ugly to improve your appearance, and your business doesn't have to be in deep trouble to improve. In fact, the ideal time to launch a *kaizen* continuous improvement initiative is when things are going well and you're happy with your outcomes. By seizing the positive, you can build on the momentum you have going, and you also have the resources and the inspiration to make a good business better. That's the key message to share with your people: we are good and we're going to get better.

Steve is charged with organizational development for a successful, multi-location food service business that has grown steadily and has been comfortably profitable. His challenge in leading an improvement crusade is that everyone has been lulled into the "why mess with success" message that is coming from his employees. They are complacent and satisfied, but Steve is inspired because he sees what they *can be*. His challenge is to sell that vision to everybody involved.

Becoming complacent is the number-one enemy of improvement. Each day you

Assignment

Create a 3 × 5 card—actually a series of them (as many as you think are necessary to reach everyone)—to post around the workplace. On them write: "We are good and we're going to get better." As you see these cards, remind your team that, though they are doing very well, they can do better. Make them a part of the improvement process by making them part of the improvement.

fail to harness the energy to be better is what we term "opportunity lost." Unfortunately, it's gone forever.

Epilogue

Sell the idea that the best time to improve your appearance is when you're looking good, and the best time to improve your business is when you're doing well.

88

How Smart People Learn

Have you been victimized by the badly misleading statement, "Experience is the best teacher"? A better truth is to say: "Experience is the most memorable teacher," because your first-hand encounter with the pain or pleasure it brings burns that memory deep into your psyche.

A productivity expert was credited with saying, "Dumb people don't learn from their mistakes." To prove that, you simply need to look at the statistics as to how many people exit prison after serving their time, and end up back in prison in a year or less (and most times for committing the same crime again). They don't learn from their experience and their mistakes. It is said smart people *do* learn from their mistakes and their experiences. If you don't believe me, ask to see the bruises, battle scars, and Purple Hearts. Again, the problem is that they experience the lesson, but don't gain the memory and what not to do the next time. That same expert said that brilliant people learn from O.P.E.—Other People's Experiences. They know that reinventing the wheel is not the best way to their success when others have already proven what they need to know.

Role models, mentors, tribal stories—there are so many resources available to help you avoid being dumb or even smart when you have the opportunity to be brilliant.

> **Assignment**
>
> Don't keep making the same mistakes, or even committing mistakes in the first place. Create a 3 × 5 card that says: "I'm an SOB: a Son Of the Business." Study your industry and your business to discover best practices and learn from them.

Epilogue

Don't be a pioneer if you don't have to. Find out what successful people do, do what they do, and you too will be successful.

89

Chasing Symptoms

Have you ever wondered why the first thing on a doctor's office visit agenda is for the nurse to take your weight, blood pressure, and pulse rate, and to ask you questions about what's wrong? What does this information have to do with the persistent cough and agonizing backache, or that stomach pain that has bugged you all week? The information gathered serves as a road map guiding your doctor from symptoms to the cause of your discomfort. Pain and changes are the body's way of telling you something is wrong.

Mark was nearly at wit's end after more than a year of trying to stem his company's slipping sales and erosion of market share. Adding to his disappointment, the company had made some positive changes in its image and marketing should have turned sales for an upswing—but didn't. In his desperate attempt to stop the pain, he had changed pay plans numerous times, offered bonuses that went without being claimed, offered awards that no one won, and gave all too many pep talks when he felt that he was only talking to himself.

After Mark called in his doctor, a consultant who specialized in human resources, he learned he had been chasing the symptoms instead of finding the real problems or the pain in his organization. The diagnosis was a near-terminal case of doubt, fear, and uncertainty among the workforce, and when he turned that around, sales turned around with it.

Assignment

On a 3 × 5 card write: "Prescription without diagnosis equals malpractice." Use this card to remind you that you need to get beyond symptoms to discover causes when something isn't working right—especially with people.

Epilogue

When confronted with problems, ask yourself if you're dealing with the symptoms or with the real illness.

125

90

You Must Know You Don't Know

If someone called you "ignorant," my bet is that you would be somewhere between hurt and devastated, or livid and furious, depending upon your emotional bent. In actuality, being ignorant can be a huge breakthrough to improvement. It can open new horizons when we understand Webster dictionary's definition of ignorance, which is "to be unlearned."

> ### *Assignment*
>
> On a 3 × 5 card write: "School is never out for the pro" (from Cavett Robert, founder of the National Speakers Association). It's okay for you or your employees to not know the answer to a question. It's not okay for you or them to fail to discover the answer. Let this card remind you of that, and use this card to talk to your team about this concept.

When a well-known CEO with a celebrated track record of inspiring change in organizations was hired by a company in deep trouble, he assembled his senior leadership team and gave them one important order. He said that any time he asked them a question, they had the right to tell him *they didn't know*, but that they would find an answer. He said the most dangerous thing they could do would be to tell him they do know, and for that to be a lie.

Today is the day to admit you know you don't know. That's when you really begin to grow. Being stupid should offend you, but being ignorant should be something you brag about. That's when learning really gets started. Ask Daniel Webster.

> **Epilogue**
>
> *It is said you can't improve anything until you're willing to admit it needs to be improved.*

91

Checklists Are a Must

Regardless of your extreme confidence or your white-knuckle fears, statistics prove that commercial air travel is the safest way to go. Per mile traveled, there are fewer accidents among commercial aircraft than there are with cars, trains, or automobiles. Why is commercial air travel is so safe? Many reasons, just one of which is the use of checklists.

When the plane is at the end of the runway and awaiting clearance to take off, the last thing the pilot and first officer do is run a checklist to make sure all of the critical issues have been handled. There's nothing worse than to be at 30,000 feet and suddenly discover you forgot to get jet fuel or, worse yet, somebody forgot to bring the air maps. You can't go back and get them.

When you find yourself agonizing and putting out fires because of consistency

---

Assignment

Create a 3 × 5 card that says: "Use checklists to maximize effectiveness." Share that with your team. Then, work with your team to create important process checklists to maximize their effectiveness. Involving them creates buy-in.

---

issues, the first step to improvement may be to creating checklists that *everyone* can follow. The key is not only to have the checklists, but to insist that they be used each and every time. For example, I use a checklist to pack for his frequent air travel to speaking engagements. This avoids arriving without socks, shoes, or underwear. You don't want to take off without fuel or maps.

Epilogue

Though you may not need a checklist for each and every series of procedures that you perform, they are invaluable where you're dealing with important issues and multiple things to remember.

92

Zero Defections and Postmortems

Our life expectancy in the United States has dramatically improved over the past decade. It can be credited to two specific sources among many: the efforts by so many people involved in healthcare, fitness, and wellness to extend both the quality and the length of people's lives; and the efforts of morticians who have used autopsies and postmortems to educate us about why people have passed away and how we might be able to prevent those conditions. It's all about education and not being afraid to see what went wrong.

The Japanese, pioneers of *kaizen* and continuous improvement, say that you can make dramatic improvements with one simple decision. You can decide that you're going to change things, and that decision alone will drive improvement. For today, I challenge you to decide that even one defection of one quality employee that could've been prevented is too many, and that by doing autopsies and postmortems on your defections, you can learn how to stop future personnel from leaving you. Set your goal on zero defections—meaning

Assignment

You might consider dividing defections of staff into three categories: those that are avoidable, those that are possibly salvageable, and those that are unavoidable (such as people who move away, have spouse issues, family problems, and so forth). Write these three categories on a 3 × 5 card for reference.

that you will not lose one employee that you should be able to keep. And if you do, you're going to learn from it in an effort to get him or her back.

Epilogue

We can't avoid death, and we can't avoid losing an employee on occasion. The key is to learn from both if we're really going to improve.

93

Consistency

Even a bad service organization is good when it can fill a customer's order on occasion. Is your order-fill consistent, or does it need improvement? A 95 percent order-fill means that

5 percent of the time you're not consistent, and you're likely to disappoint a customer.

When Beth accepted the challenge of managing an inventory with thousands of SKUs (stock-keeping units), her ultimate mission was to make customers smile. Her salespeople wanted to be consistent with uttering those magic words: "Yes, ma'am (or yes, sir). We've got it in stock and you can take it with you now."

Assignment

On a 3 × 5 card, write: "Involve me and I'll be part of the solution. Dictate to me or ignore me and I'll be part of the problem." When solving problems and challenges, involve your key team members. They know the business, too, and their involvement in the process will energize the solution. Review this card any time you have a problem to resolve.

Her second mission was bolstering morale and inspiring her salespeople by eliminating the excuses and apologies they were making about stockage failures in today's "I need it now" world. Her mission was to improve consistency and their ability to say yes, with the ultimate goal of gaining and retaining customers.

How did she do it, you ask? She worked with sales to discover what was commonly requested and then made certain they had those SKUs on hand all the time. This was a constant battle, because SKUs and customer needs often changed. So, she kept the sales folks in the loop constantly. And they appreciated that enormously.

Epilogue

Involve team members in finding solutions. When they help resolve a problem, they become part of the solution and buy in. They also know you value their role, opinions, and experience.

94

Your Hall of Fame

Try to imagine the immense pride any player nominated to the baseball or football hall of fame must feel. Try to picture the glow on his face when he sees his name among the legendary few to ever win that honor. Putting your people in the spotlight can improve everyone's spirit and especially inspire the customers at the receiving end of your hall-of-fame-class service.

One Chicago office supply wholesaler has made its hall of fame concept really pay off. It adds the person's name to its hall of fame roster, sometimes multiple times, to recognize that employee. This system is a result of customers who write complementary letters for the exceptional customer service and specifically name that employee.

This company gives the employee a cash award and a written congratulations. Talk about inspiring people—cash talks! These customer service letters and their hall-of-fame names are posted in their customer waiting area.

> ### *Assignment*
>
> On a 3 × 5 card, write: "What gets rewarded gets repeated." You can create your own hall of fame and improvise the ideas that your team might brainstorm. The important thing is to recognize and put people in the spotlight.

Employees not only are inspired by this recognition, they try to excel at customer service so they may be honored again and again, and customers get the message that when they get great service, they should write a letter that would be both appreciated and valued.

Epilogue
The motivational principle of "what gets rewarded gets repeated" is the driving force behind creating your hall of fame.

95

Your Wall of Shame

Why is it no one talks about shame? No matter how hard you try, no matter how committed you are, and no matter how much you work to improve, on occasion you're going to encounter a speed bump in serving customers. There are so many possible perils in the service process and so many outside forces just waiting to derail your best intentions that it is a fact that mistakes will be made. It is a shame.

Assignment

On a 3 × 5 card write, "Set up a Wall of Shame." Then actually set one up, using 3 × 5 cards with stories on them as a visual reminder of things that went wrong in the past. It'll be a reminder for everyone to avoid them in the future. NOTE: This wall should be constructed out of customers' sight.

In all of history, there has never been more thought, engineering, analysis, planning, and commitment of resources given to anything such as we have given to NASA for the manned space program. Yet with all of the very best in the world, we've had accidents and deaths. Even the best of the best can't stop those occasional glitches in a system. It's the same with service delivery.

However, acknowledging that they happen doesn't mean they are acceptable. Everyone on the team must become involved in identifying them, analyzing them, and trying to keep them from happening again.

Epilogue

The first time you have a problem, it can be called an accident. The second and each additional time, it can be called your fault.

96

The Oxen Principle

Have you ever noticed how easy it is to make something that is incredibly simple really complicated? Often, training agendas become so seemingly complex that they get swept aside in favor of other priorities. Here is one of the simplest and most effective training principles you can implement in your company, regardless of your size.

Thousands of years ago, the Chinese found that the "Oxen Principle" was incredibly simple and amazingly effective for training. When they had a new ox to train, they would simply yoke that ox with one already trained, one that knew how to work and had been there for a while, and let the trained ox teach the newcomer. The seasoned oxen knew when to pull, when to rest, and when to head to the barn. Before long, the newcomer realized that the simple thing to do was go along with the plan. In a few weeks, both oxen had the same training agenda.

When you want to teach a new hire the basics, or you want to upgrade someone's skills, find willing oxen within your company—people who enjoy training and are good at it—and tether them to the person you want to train. It's amazingly simple, it's quick, and it works.

Assignment

On a 3 × 5 card, write: "The basic framework of every training program is:

1. What result do we want?
2. What standards must be met to achieve the desired result?
3. What training will ensure the standards are met?"

Then write down the names of key employees who can serve as trainers. Use this card when you need to set up a training program.

Epilogue

When you select a seasoned ox to train a newcomer, be sure the one doing the training is doing it your way.

97

Satisfaction: The Kiss of Death!

Many companies' training goal is to produce customer satisfaction. Today's more demanding customers require you to raise the bar far beyond satisfied. Your training should produce a customer outcome that is "delighted," customers who want to buy again and who see you as their first preference when making their next buying choice.

When Marcy called the plumbing firm for a commode that had been stopped up, the plumber had the problem repaired within 30 minutes. He asked her if the second bathroom commode or sink needed any adjustments or work, because the company had a one-hour minimum. She commented, "No, the other commode worked perfectly, although it flushed a little slow." The plumber went in, checked it, and found that the water level was low. Indeed, it was flushing slow. It had been that way for six years since they bought the house. At the end of the service call, Marcy ended up with two bathrooms that were working perfectly and a smile on her face. She will cling to that company, because the plumber went beyond satisfied to *delighted*.

Assignment

On a 3 × 5 card, write: "My team needs to go beyond satisfied customers to delighted customers. And it's my responsibility to lead them to that level of service." Use the card to remind you not only what the goal is, but also who's responsible for achieving it.

Epilogue

Today, with demanding customers and a competitor around very corner, you must set your goals higher to produce those delighted customers.

98

Correct Your Thinking = Retraining

There's a huge misunderstanding about training. Whether you are training five or 500 people, start by recognizing that everyone is already trained. Your real effort is to "retrain" them to follow *your* processes and procedures, and obtain *your* desired outcomes. Some people are trained to do it very similarly to what you want, and some will appear to have been beamed in from another planet. Training is necessary to get everyone following very similar thinking and procedures.

A California manufacturer struggled with their training until managers realized that what they were really trying to do was to change human behavior: to change thinking processes,

Assignment

On a 3 × 5 card, write the following guidance: "Good training is actually retraining. Get them thinking and moving to the beat of our drum, not someone else's drum." That's the heart of training today. Use this card to remind you of this when you set up training programs.

to rethink habits, and to focus on different outcomes. That is the reason all military training begins with the basics. They know the challenge is to get out with the old and in with the new, starting with the thinking process and, at the same time, reinforcing the new behaviors and actions.

Epilogue

If you've ever tried to "retrain" yourself for a habit such as smoking, overeating, or changing your language, you know retraining takes time and reinforcement.

99

Keyoka

Once again, the Japanese help us with that important term that can make your training efforts incredibly effective. The Japanese term *keyoka* means "we shall have one set of eyes." For our training purposes, that means our goal is to have everyone striving for common and well-defined outcomes. Without giving them a vision of the one set of eyes that you want, five different people will end up producing five different results. *Keyoka* gets everybody on the same page.

After visiting eight different locations for a northeastern wholesaler, I was dumbfounded by how different eight stores could be, yet they fly the same flag for the same company. There was little similarity in their signage, inventories, displays, housekeeping, policies, and procedures, and in how they went about customer service. After some intense study, we found that every manager had a different set of eyes. Each was doing his or her own thing and arriving at different end results. This problem made consistent customer service almost impossible. It made internal operations inconsistent, and it was a disaster for the company's profits. The solution was to teach everybody to have one set of eyes.

Assignment

The best way to create this "one set of eyes" is to establish a model against which everyone can measure and compare their performances. On a 3 × 5 card, write: "I will create a *keyoka* philosophy by modeling the behaviors I expect to set the example."

Epilogue

Think of keyoka *as a picture frame that surrounds what you want to accomplish. Then, within that picture frame, you can allow your people to be empowered and individualize their own approaches.*

100

Your ABCs and 1,000 Little Things

Your first days in school were spent learning the fundamentals of the English language: your ABCs. Only then could you move on to learn the 1,000 other things that were important, but only doable if you had committed your ABCs to memory. We can follow that same successful logic in designing any training procedure. Little things can become big things.

Recently, a friend told me about trying to sleep at a summer camp where there was one lonely mosquito that kept buzzing around his head. He said he couldn't believe that a 200-pound person could be so intimidated by such a tiny little mosquito. Finally, he turned the light on and killed that sucker, and life got better.

> ## Assignment
>
> On a 3 × 5 card, write: "Remember the 1,000 Little Things." Post it visibly so everyone can see it to remind them to pay attention to the details.

You've undoubtedly done a good job at managing the big things in your company—you've learned your ABCs. Now you can work on the 1,000 little things. All too often, businesses overlook the little things, thinking they're not all that important. But to the employee who has one little thing they need, such as getting off early, getting help with his or her health insurance, or dealing with somebody who knows what he or she is doing, that little thing becomes huge and can be a barrier in inspiring people. When you get the big things perfected, it's time to turn to the little things and manage the details. It's the polish that will retain and inspire people.

> ### Epilogue
> *Rarely is there just one thing that attracts a superstar employee to join you. Normally, it's a combination of many things done consistently and done well that wins his or her heart and gets him or her to stick with you through thick and thin.*

101

Green Is Growing; Red Is Rotting

Are you aware that those tomatoes in your grocery store were picked green from some faraway, warm climate and shipped in to be sold in your area? Upon arrival, they are put through a gassing process that turns them red. That's why they often look decent on the outside, and on the inside, they're yellow and hard. People are often similar to tomatoes: when we're green, we're growing—and the moment we turn red, we begin to rot. In our case, rot means that we stagnate and stop learning. Experts tell us that the average person may accumulate knowledge over his or her lifetime, but people really end their learning curve in their early 20s.

Assignment

Keeping yourself up to date is important. You have to keep your training and education up to date to be effective with your team. On a 3 × 5 card, write: "I am also part of the working team and need training myself." Then schedule some professionally enhancing training for yourself.

Cavitt Robert, founder of the National Speakers Association, taught the principle that we should be involved in lifelong learning. He said that school is never out for the pro. When is the last time you finished a really good book on marketing, reviewed a DVD on customer service, or attended a seminar on the cutting edge of technology? If you've gotten into a rut, it's time to challenge yourself and get green again.

Epilogue

How can you expect your employees to be up to date if you are not? You have a responsibility to yourself to keep learning and growing.

102

Teacher, Preacher, Coach, or Shrink?

What is your role in training? That probably varies, depending on whether you're a business owner, who does on-the-job training while carrying on 100 other tasks, or you use a corporate trainer, who makes training a full-time venture. Regardless of your answer, research has shown there are four roles you must play in an effective training program.

A famous pizza chain has a philosophy: Your job is to make it, bake it, take it, or support someone who does—four clear roles in getting that pizza delivered to the customer's door. In the process of training, you will find yourself being a *teacher*, a *preacher*, a *coach*, and a *shrink*.

Your role as a teacher is to make sure that people know the thinking processes and the skills that they need to be successful on the job.

Assignment

"I am a teacher, preacher, a coach, and a shrink." Write that on a 3 x 5 card and post it in your office somewhere prominent. It will remind you of your four roles in training.

141

Your role as a preacher is to spread enthusiasm everywhere you go to get people fired up and inspired, to use the training as it's taught. Your role as a coach is to constantly critique the results they are getting and encourage your players to make adjustments, as needed. A coach's job is 24/7. And last, your job is to be a shrink: to analyze people, processes, and outcomes and to recommend changes when they're appropriate. And in that role and in training, you will need to get inside people's heads to be effective.

Epilogue
The mediocre teacher tells. The good teacher explains. The superior teacher demonstrates. The great teacher inspires.

103

A Different Approach to Communication: Using "McMeetings"

Leadership is about creating a business environment where training succeeds by supporting and challenging people to be their best. That environment should inspire people to participate. One of the challenges is to communicate, especially one on one, with your key staff.

One CEO was given a certificate, supposedly from the Fast Food Conference Rooms of America. This was obviously a phrase created by his employees because he often asked his staff to join him at a local McDonald's or coffee shop when he had some important communication to go over with them. He saved these times to manage the critical few. By escaping from his office, he was able to give the person or people he met with 100 percent attention with no mental distractions around them, showing those joining him that they were important and that he was not going to allow interruptions to destroy their "McMeeting."

Perhaps your company should be like his, and use your conference room to have lunch and escape periodically with key people when you want to communicate very important issues, ideas, and challenges.

Assignment

Write on a 3 × 5 card: "Communication: (1) The greatest problem with communication is to assume it took place. (2) Communication, or the message, is always in the mind of the receiver. Doing key communication one on one is my goal."

Epilogue

Time has become crucial, and you should consider this one-on-one idea at your local coffee shop. Perhaps you'll be given a certificate from the Fast Food Conference Rooms of America.

104

The Hidden Payoff in Training Events

When the management of a large warehouse operation improved the lighting and made things brighter in the warehouse, they were excited to learn that productivity went up almost 18 percent. Upon analysis, it wasn't attributed to the fact that people could see better. Instead, it was a feeling that they were cared about, and management was making it easier and better for them to work. The change inspired them.

Some months later, a change of management decided to turn the lighting back down. Guess what happened? Productivity went up again. Why? Because they were perceived as paying attention to their people. Folks working in the warehouse believed that management was making the changes because they were important. That is one of the hidden outcomes of training.

At times, you might pick one of your people to go through training simply to inspire him or her and to raise his or her self-esteem. Participation in training, particularly events outside the company, can pay off regardless of the topic or what your employee learns. It's paying attention and caring about people.

> **Assignment**
>
> "Sending employees to external training opportunities has a hidden benefit beyond just the training: it communicates that the employee is important and valued to our organization." Write this on a 3 × 5 card to review on occasion.

Epilogue

Caring creates caring, and your people can't transfer good feelings to your customers unless they get those good feelings from you.

105

Uncle F.E.S.S.

This Uncle F.E.S.S. training idea starts with the 80-20 rule, better known as the "Pareto Principle." In 1906, Vilfredo Pareto, an Italian economist, found that 20 percent of something is always responsible for 80 percent of the results. For example, 20 percent of your inventory will create 80 percent or more of your sales.

When an Atlanta sign company tackled excessive employee turnover, it found a lack of training, and the 80-20 rule was generating stress, anxiety, and frustration for its telephone people. Of its product and service inquiries, complaints and questions equaled 80 percent of what the telephone people were dealing with. Only 20 percent were product orders. Next, the company brainstormed answers to the 10 most popular calls and actually

Assignment

After some research, write on a 3 × 5 card your top 10 Uncle F.E.S.S. issues—which 20 percent of activities are taking 80 percent of the time available. Brainstorm with your team and possibly outsiders some solutions. Record those solutions and then implement them.

ended up with scripts, some key words, and some answers that were predetermined before the phone rang. Now, the telephone people could simply go to a flip index to answer inquiries, complaints, and questions, and do it consistently. It reduced stress, made everybody happier, and inspired both employees and customers. And it also reduced employee turnover.

Epilogue

The expertise of your employees to identify and repair these 80-20 problems not only helps fix the problems, but makes them part of the solution.

106

Do You Have Reasons—Or Excuses?

The cruelest punishment you can give another person is to hold him or her in solitary confinement, to not communicate with him or her. In prisons, it's called "The Hole," and prisoners are isolated from everyone else. Some say that an extended stay in solitary confinement can even cause mental illness. For the purpose of this idea, we want to focus on why you don't give enough compliments to your people.

There's a phrase used in State Department and diplomatic circles called *persona non grata*, which means you are an "unwelcome person," and that's the way many of your employees feel when they've done a good job and fail to hear from you. Just remember that the failure to communicate subjects your employee to that solitary confinement. That is what you're doing when you don't recognize and respect what he or she has accomplished. Make a commitment today that you're going to give many more compliments beginning this very day and into the future.

When one employee was asked when the last time he got a compliment from management was, he asked what year it was.

> ## Assignment
>
> On a 3 × 5 card, write: "I will catch my employees being good and hand out sincere compliments every day." Review this card routinely.

Epilogue

Make a decision about what you want reinforced, and then do it with your compliments. Don't keep your people in the dark.

107

What Is True Empowerment?

All too often, what many call empowerment is actually simple delegation, or even dumping. Everyone needs to understand that management techniques are not magic mantras, but simply tools to be reached for at the right times. One of those tools is to truly empower your people. If you claim to empower them but hold back their right to make decisions, you confuse them, reduce your credibility, and drain your organization's resources.

When handing over empowerment situations, the key is to define what needs to be done, define the outcome you are looking for, and explain why that outcome is important. If you want to add any suggestions or tips for getting the job done easily or quickly, or for getting a better end result, do so. But then allow the employees themselves to figure out the "how" of getting it done.

Often, management fails to empower people because they're afraid they'll screw up. If it's crucial, then you can agree it's probably a good principle. However, there are many, many things that you can empower people to do that will help them grow in confidence and be more ready to take on the next assignment.

Assignment

"Empowerment means giving up the authority to make decisions, not just execute orders without supervision." Write this on a 3 × 5 card and review it weekly to remind yourself of what true empowerment really is.

Epilogue

There's nothing more demeaning than to be told you are empowered to do something, and then have management hold back the decision-making authority.

108

MMFI

One thing is critical in the creation and operation of a company that has long-term, sustainable success. It's the thing that makes a difference between good and great. It is the thing that makes a difference between a few good years and many great years. It is the issue of how employees are treated on a day-to-day basis.

Mary Kay Ash said, "There are two things people want more than sex and money...recognition and praise." When people feel valued and appreciated, they are more productive. The company is more competitive and in a better position to treat its people well, and so on. It's a virtuous circle. Yet treating people well is surprisingly uncommon in Corporate America today.

Assignment

Post a 3 × 5 card in your office where you will see it routinely on which you've written: "MMFI: Make Me Feel Important." Use it to remind yourself that people respond best when they feel valued. Make your employees feel valued.

Decide right now that you're going to put your people on a pedestal and make them feel important. By doing so, you can also get to know their needs, their wants, their goals, and their dreams.

Epilogue

Everyone needs to be appreciated and respected, and get a pat on the back occasionally.

109

Card Everyone

Sometimes, the simplest and least expensive ideas can have the greatest payoff. When it comes to inspiring and recognizing people, there is nothing simpler than having every person who works for you to have business cards. They are inexpensive and give incredible meaning to some people, especially those who have never had them.

For this tiny investment, your people will be proud to leave their cards with every customer and every prospect. They'll hand out those cards to friends and relatives, and your business will have its name in many unexpected places at little cost. That card will talk for you and, because you've made them feel important, your employees will be promoting your company, and that is powerful.

Assignment

On a 3 × 5 card, so you don't forget, write: "Business Cards for All!" Then get business cards for every employee. Set up an electronic file account with your local Kinko's or printers, so the format will be done and available. Add the person's name and title, and they're ready to go. Try to have business cards for employees on their first day of work.

Epilogue

Business cards communicate to employees a sense of belonging and of being part of the team. They also demonstrate your real and personal interest in them.

110

Feel the Fear

To understand what inspires people, we also need to understand what causes them to perform at a lower level than might be possible. The phrase to remember is "limiting fears." Think of a speed limit. People get to 55 mph, and that's as fast as they will go. They are afraid to go faster. The greatest roadblocks to high performance are fear and anxiety, and they can actually incapacitate a person.

We see fear played out most with salespeople. They have the fear of rejection when, in actuality, they are not being rejected; they are being refused. To understand fear, we need to break down the word. *Fear* means "false expectations appearing real." Is fear a friend or foe? Fear, at the right time and in the right dose, can be healthy. It can warn us and protect us. However, most fears are irrational, and they come from negative outcomes in the mind.

Assignment

Write down some of the things you fear. Your employees fear many of the same things. On a 3 × 5 card, write: "Fear is false expectations appearing real. I'll help by employees over fear by encouragement and a willingness to accept their fears leading to small failures if they are willing to try." Then encourage them to risk the things they are fearful of.

To inspire people, you also need to be an encourager. The only way you can conquer fear is to inspire and encourage your people to take a bite out of it, or to try. Unfortunately, there's no other fix. But as they experience successes with the things they fear, fear goes away. If you know you can overcome what you're fearful of, you neutralize it. You are no longer vulnerable.

> **Epilogue**
>
> *As an encourager and a teacher, remind your people that most of what they fear, particularly in selling, is not fear at all. They are simply being refused. That takes the power out of fear.*

111

They Don't Know How Much You Care

Virtually every company in America talks about how important its employees are, but then fails to prove it. People don't care how much you know until they know how much you care.

It's easy to talk, but the challenge is to show them.

When a massive fire nearly destroyed the Malden Mills Manufacturing Company in Massachusetts, 3,000 employees were certain they would be out of work. Their CEO astonished them when he announced he would keep all 3,000 of his employees on the payroll and start rebuilding the 90-year-old family business. He paid them for a month, and then a second month, and then a third month, until the plant was reopened. He said the fundamental difference between him and most other CEOs

> **Assignment**
>
> True caring is demonstrated, not spoken. On a 3 × 5 card, write: "At my next opportunity, I will show my team I care about them in some way. And I'll do that at least once a month." Then do it. Review this card once each month to remind yourself of your commitment.

is that he considers his workers an asset and not an expense. However, this is where he showed them, not just talked.

Epilogue

People repaid this CEO's support and caring by almost doubling their productivity. Everyone was a winner.

112

Forget Telling: Show Them You Love Them

Again, do you know how many opportunities there are to show your people you care? For sure, there are 365 (and every four years, 366 opportunities). That's how many days there are on your calendar, and every day you may have a chance to both tell and show your people how important they are to you.

Turn your planning book, your Rolodex, or your Palm Pilot into a recognition machine. You can keep track of birthdays, anniversaries, the dates people joined the company, weddings, births, the ages and birthdays of children, recognition of people winning special events, and participating in traveling. The list is endless. Think of each day as an opportunity to show, not just tell, people you care. Celebrate. Use cakes and ice cream and all kinds of creative ways to demonstrate to them that you do more than just talk.

Assignment

Return to your set of employee cards. On each employee's card, write down his or her birthday, anniversary, employment anniversary, kids' birthdays—anything you can discover. Your HR records will have much of this. Ask for the rest. Then, use this information to demonstrate that you care by doing simple things: send a card; make an announcement at work; take the employee to lunch. The options are endless. Just do something.

Epilogue

The principal way to stand out in a crowd is to be different, and you will be different if you truly use these milestones and events as opportunities to celebrate.

113

Friendly and Firm, but Is It Fair?

One of the great struggles for any good leader, CEO, or manager is to attempt to be fair with his or her subordinates. However, the problem is what's good for the goose may not be good for the gander. In other words, "fair" can have a different meaning to every person. In your attempt to be fair, you need a thinking process, and here it is.

Coach John Wooden, the winningest coach in college basketball, was known for his famous quote: "I treat everybody fair, but not equal." His point was that when people contribute more, they should get more from the outcome. When people accomplish more, they should be rewarded more. That is in both dollars and benefits.

> **Assignment**
>
> On a 3 × 5 card write: "Reward those who deserve rewards. Be fair but not equal."

Epilogue

The United States is a place where everyone has the equal right to be unequal.

114

Little p, Big E

Once again, the Japanese and their business principles can serve as role models for us. They are incredibly diligent about planning and believe that is one of the reasons they've been able to dominate many business categories around the world. They believe that American businesses are too busy shooting from the hip and not thinking through the new things they attempt.

Dick, CEO of a Chicago publishing company, says he has seen many companies fail in his lifetime of business experience. He has never seen a company fail because it did too much planning, but he's seen many companies fail because they do too little planning.

The Japanese believe that we use the little p and the big E, and they do just the opposite, and that's our recommendation to you when you think about inspiring and involving people. The big P is for planning. Take your time to make a good plan, and when you roll out your little e—execution—you have thought through the resources you need, the problems you might have, and the people it will take to make your plan work.

> ### Assignment
>
> Planning leads to excellent execution (little e), and you owe your team good planning (the big P). You should also involve them in that planning to ensure its success. On a 3 × 5 card, write: "To fail to plan is to plan to fail." Review the card occasionally to remind yourself how important planning is to your, and their, success.

Epilogue

By adopting the big P and little e, you will avoid many of the casualties that come about from a lack of planning.

115

They Must Agree: A Willing Spirit

You can't push people! Show me a manager who has tried to push people into doing what he or she wants done, and I'll show you someone who has probably caved in to using threats and intimidation, or tried to buy his or her way with incentive pay and benefits. They don't work! They are both external motivators, and the moment you take those motivators away, the behavior stops.

Former president Dwight Eisenhower was legendary for his "piece of string" story. When he had military subordinates who were getting black marks because they were pushing people, threatening people, and using intimidation, he would call them into his office. He would hand them a short piece of string and ask them to push the string across his desk. Obviously, when doing that, the string wads up in a

---

Assignment

To help you remember the pull vs. push idea, write the following on a 3 × 5 card: "Push the string and it wads up. Pull the string and it cooperates." Review this card when you need to motivate your team or an individual employee.

---

ball, just as people wad up and refuse to cooperate. He would then show the subordinates the importance of pulling people and being an encourager and an inspirer, not a pusher.

William James, a famous European writer, said that the number-one ingredient to get people to cooperate with you is a willing spirit. The key words when you want something done are "*I need your help.*" Don't lose sight of them, and be an encourager, not a pusher.

> ### Epilogue
> *Think back to your childhood and how you reacted to fear and intimidation. With that in mind, you will never use them again because they will deliver a total failure.*

116

The Magic Question: What Do You Think?

How many times have you had problems, or hit roadblocks, or had something totally derailed because you didn't have the information you needed and you didn't do the research you should have done? Why are we afraid to ask other people for their opinions? All too often, we think it makes us appear to be small and trivial, and that we're not capable of making our own decisions. However, the really smart businessperson uses the four most important words in the English language.

Kop Kopmeyer had a sign in his office that said, "The four most important words in the world." And underneath that, it said, "What do you think?" He knew that when you ask, you learn. When you ask, you grow. When you ask, you get information and other opinions to help you make better decisions. Do you need to join the world of askers?

When you ask people what they think, be very careful to give credit where credit is due. Let it be their idea, not yours. Also, if people give you good input and good ideas and you don't react to them, it's often wise to get back to them and let

Assignment

Make an "ask" sign on a 3 x 5 card with the four most important words: "What do you think?" Review this card routinely.

them know why it wasn't a fit or why you can't do it right now. What gets rewarded gets repeated. Don't forget to thank people, both verbally and perhaps tangibly, when they've given you good information.

Epilogue

Mr. Kopmeyer said, *"The solution to every problem is out there if we just develop the courage and the habit and the discipline of asking."*

117

How to Follow the "Wise Judge Principle" in Dealing With People

Have you ever had someone accuse you about something that happened, in which the information from which they were operating was totally wrong? If you make decisions about issues such as mistakes, discipline, and problems, there's a huge opportunity to misjudge or reach misdirected conclusions. Sometimes we need to go into the courtroom to understand one core principle that we need to apply here.

When police officers investigate serious accidents or crimes, one of the first things they do is interview all available witnesses involved in that situation. One police officer said he was always awed because he could interview two people who saw the exact same accident at the same time at the same corner, and they would have totally different descriptions of what happened. The challenge is to sort out the truth. A wise judge always listens to all parties involved before making a decision.

So the next time you're about to jump on your people or accuse them, make sure that you have heard everybody, and then try to arrive at a fair conclusion. It's hard to seek out the truth sometimes, even when you have all the facts. What's going

Assignment

Remember the "Wise Judge Principle" when handling personnel issues. On a 3 × 5 card, write: "Be a wise judge. Doubt the initial information I receive until I can validate it. Then render a fair judgment."

to happen if you don't have the clear facts? Such uninformed decisions douse inspiration like a fireman pouring water on a fire.

Epilogue

Nothing is more demeaning or downgrading to an employee than to be challenged about something when he or she is innocent.

118

Your Door Is Open

Have you heard "the lights are on, but nobody's home"? It's hard to remember how many times I've been told that an employer has an open-door policy, but upon further inspection, I find an open door and a closed mind. Everyone in life operates from a different memory bank shaped by the events in their lives. The challenge in working with people is not allowing those past experiences, prejudices, perceptions, predispositions, and predictions to roadblock our thinking.

As I delivered my consulting report for a multilocation Detroit business, the chairman of the board

Assignment

Make your open door policy also mean an "open mind" policy. Don't let preconceived notions and ideas block new ideas and information. On your next 3 × 5 card, write: "Open Door—Open Mind." Review as needed.

gave me high marks for my analysis and recommendations

161

to reshape the company. He went on to explain that he absolutely believed that the course of action I had laid out would both work and have a huge payoff for his company. However, he said, "I'm just not willing to make those changes and do what it takes to follow the course of action you have outlined." Within six months, this well-established family business had filed for bankruptcy and was gone. He had an open door but a closed mind.

Epilogue

A mind is a horrible thing to waste. If you're not open-minded, you simply have hired a body and you're not really listening to the wealth of ideas and information others can bring to your open door.

119

Weasel Words

One necessary ingredient to keep the human spirit alive is hope—hope that tomorrow will be a better day, and hope for the future. By adopting a policy of promoting from within, you afford your all-star employees the hope, inspiration, and opportunity they need to go above and beyond, and earn the opportunity to move up. At the same time, you can lock yourself into a self-made prison by making absolute promises about promoting from within.

From the founding of IBM (International Business Machines), Thomas Watson followed the policy that IBM would promote from within. For decades IBM did exactly that.

Then, in recent years, as it's had to reinvent itself to stay alive in the market, it brought in three people from the outside. This shook the very foundations of IBM, and the ripple effect went through the company. Bringing someone in from the outside was just unheard of, and IBM got caught because it had locked itself into an unofficial policy of promoting from within. Be on guard from this experience to protect yourself.

When stipulating that you will promote from within, use weasel words such as "we would prefer to...," " "it

Assignment

Always advertise the open jobs both internally and externally, and make everyone aware of that. Although you should prefer to hire from within, it may not work out that way every time. On a 3 × 5 card, write: "Hire from within except when I can't get what I need from within."

is our desire if the manpower is available...," and such to set a condition that you could bring someone in from the outside if he or she were better qualified than your existing employees. In that way, you actually create a competition for people to want to move up.

Epilogue

Don't be "hung by the tongue" with your own words and get locked into a situation where you have no options.

163

120

A Family Affair

If you're involved or work for a family-owned or -run business, you know that can be the thrill of victory or the agony of defeat. Though a family business can offer a unique opportunity to form relationships and gain respect and rewards that a family normally couldn't do, it can also be a nightmare if family members aren't committed to cooperation.

Assignment

If you are part of a family-owned business, consider outside help when appropriate. Outsiders can often get beyond family relationships to real truths. On a 3 × 5 card, write: "In a family-owned business, there is a time for external consultants. Is now one of those times?"

Mike Henning is probably the most respected family business consultant in the country, and if you can sit and just listen to some of the stories he can tell about the pitfalls, perils, and problems that can arise from family businesses, it's enough to scare you to death.

For this quick idea, the challenge is to put aside your selfishness and be on guard for greed, pride, and arrogance as forces that can rip your business apart. You need an attitude of cooperation and consideration for others to make it work, and it can.

Epilogue
Your family business can be a really meaningful experience if everyone involved realizes that money and stuff are not the goal, and that people are what is important, both inside and outside your business. Work to inspire others.

121

Your Greatest Challenge: Egocentric

Perhaps our great single obstacle to success is getting out of the way and parking our egos at the curb. An ego is a necessary and valuable driving force for success, but it can also be very destructive when our egos get out of control and we think we are better than other people.

Assignment

On a 3 × 5 card, remind yourself of the importance of involving your employees. Write: "Tell me, and I will forget; show me, and I may remember; but *involve* me, and I will understand." Review as needed.

Here is a powerful quote from a bulletin board in a business employee break-room. Think about the message and how you can apply it with your people.

"Tell me, and I will forget; show me, and I may remember; but *involve* me, and I will understand."

Involvement is a necessary ingredient in building teamwork and pulling people in to be part of your mission and vision for the future. There are many ways to involve people, and your challenge is to read back through this book to pick out some of those that support this quote.

Epilogue

When you pull your people in and get them truly involved, the payoff will exceed your wildest expectations. Just get over your ego to do it.

122

The Only Thing That Works When People Are Off-Track

One thing we know about trains is that, on occasion, they derail, and the outcome can be tragic: locomotives lying on the ground, cars piled everywhere, and people hurt or killed. Your people are much the same. They occasionally become derailed, get off-track, lose interest in the job and even in their personal lives. Your role as an inspirer is to encourage them to get back on track, but the question is how to do it. In fact, that is Excedrin headache number one through 25 for most managers.

W. Clement Stone became one of America's first billionaires as a result of building a company called Combined Insurance. His method for becoming incredibly wealthy was to hire thousands and thousands of people to sell his inexpensive insurance policies. He was one of the first in the country to use scripts and to insist that everyone follow them. Used right, their sales success was virtually guaranteed. However, he also knew that even great people sometimes get off-track and need help. Over the years, he found that the only way to get them

> **Assignment**
>
> Know your people and know their goals so you can help them get back on-track when they need that help. Review your employee 3 × 5 cards to ensure that you have recorded the goals your employees have set for themselves so you can remind them when they get off track. If you haven't captured that information, now is a good time to have that discussion.

really back on track was to remind them that they were hurting themselves by not working to achieve their personal goals and objectives. In other words, getting them back on track is all about them.

Epilogue

It is human to lose sight of where we want to go, and we need help and encouragement to get back on track.

123

Winston's Wisdom: Your Best Is Not Enough

One of the hot topics in business today is how to go from good to great. It is no longer enough to be good, because all your competitors are good. Your leadership role is to create a company atmosphere where people really *want* to excel.

Winston Churchill became legendary during World War II for his ability to rally people. One of his quotes that can really fire up your enthusiasm when everything seems to overwhelm you is the following: "Sometimes it is not enough to do your best. You must do what is required."

Assignment

On a 3 × 5 card, write down Churchill's quote: "Sometimes it is not enough to do your best. You must do what is required." Occasionally review it and share it with your team.

Think about that quote when you're burned out, tired, or just ready to give up. It seems to just reach down inside and

167

inspire us to make that additional effort to do that little bit more. Winston's quote can be your ticket to getting everyone involved to do what it takes to succeed in business today, because sometimes your best is not enough.

Epilogue

Churchill was a master motivator. You can be, too, by following his commonsense approach to inspiring people.

124

Fringe Benefits

It is somewhere between difficult and impossible to be inspired about delivering great customer service when your mind is cluttered with fear and worry about paying for a hospital stay, or how to deal with doctor bills that are piling up, or your check being short because you were out sick.

Rod Reason, president of Total Benefits Company, points out that benefits are not a motivator of people, but the lack of fringe benefits can be a de-motivator of people. Today, more than ever, people are aware of the need for health insurance, a 401(k),

Assignment

The lack of benefits is a de-motivator. Counterproductive. On a 3 × 5 card, write: "Benefits are important parts of the compensation package. But they don't provide motivation. Employees need them and expect them." Review this card every time you think about changing your benefits package.

and long-term disability. If you can't provide those, people may well end up working for your competitor down the street.

Start today by seeing benefits as an opportunity to retain people and truly get them involved in the job.

Epilogue

Benefits have become one of the greatest retention tools you can use. The next time you're due to give a raise, you might improve fringe benefits.

125

Retention: Annual Revenues Stink

Try to picture a boss or supervisor who's unhappy with some aspect of your job performance but waits almost a year to review it with you. What a tragedy. All too often, annual performance reviews become "save up and zap" sessions where managers download on the people they're reviewing. They rip the meat from the bones and demoralize the folks being reviewed.

Mark, a senior manager at Cisco Systems, is required to do an annual review for each of his employees. In actuality, he does two reviews. The first

Assignment

Make your performance reviews meaningful and useful. On a 3 × 5 card, write the following: "Performance reviews are as much to coach as to review. Do them as needed, not once a year." Put this card in front of the employee cards to remind you. Remember to use your employee performance cards.

one is for corporate; it contains all the typical language about the employee really trying and improving and so on. Then he does a second review, which is in reality the one he uses to help plan the next year with each employee. When he calls each person in for an annual review, they talk about what they accomplished in the past year and how Mark can help that person be more successful the next year.

In the military, a kiss of death is to get an annual review that says you did a "good" job. This is particularly true if you plan to stay in the service. To remain in today's military, you must get a review that says you've done an "excellent" to "awesome" job, or you are gone.

Epilogue

Turn on the lights and acknowledge people's strengths, weaknesses, and concerns on a daily basis.

126

You Should Be Arrested!

Imagine yourself working day in and day out without a word that your performance was substandard, and the first time you learning that management was unhappy was when they called you in and fired you. All too often managers form an invisible agreement between them and their subordinates that no news is good news. Then, out of the clear blue, they'll dismiss someone without ever giving the person a chance to improve his or her performance.

At a plastics plant in my hometown, a worker was called to the office, and three of the management people berated him and talked to him as if he were a dog, and ended up firing him. Prior to that, he had no hint that they were unhappy with his performance. He went home enraged and devastated, and went back to the plastics plant with a sawed-off shotgun. Late that night, three managers from the plastics company were in the morgue with a tag on their toe. He got revenge. He didn't get mad; he got even.

You should be keeping your employees informed about their performances, both good and bad. If you're guilty of not doing that, change it today.

Assignment

Record the following on a 3 × 5 card: "Employees should get a chance to improve their performance. They need to know:

1.   What's unacceptable.

2.   What the standard is and what managment expects them to do to fix it.

3.   The timetable and how it's going to be measured."

Epilogue

The way you treat outbound employees sends a huge message to the remaining group as to how they might be treated in the future.

127

If They Need a
Raise, Fire the Boss

If you believe inspiration, great leadership, and a package of fringe benefits will keep people on the job, try telling your people that you really care about them and that they are important to you, but that you will no longer be able to pay them. Effective immediately, there will be no more paychecks, but you would sure like everybody to stick around and continue to do their work. How many of your employees do you think will still be on the job late today?

J.R., a seasoned business owner and inspirational leader, believed paychecks were his opportunity to show his people a tangible way that their work was appreciated. He also believed that employees should never come to him to ask for a raise—that he should be proactive and keep them apprised of all that the company could afford to pay them. Asking for a raise often feels like begging, and it is demeaning and stressful for your people. Become someone who keeps them informed and offers them performance reviews frequently, along with raises when appropriate.

> ### Assignment
>
> On a 3 × 5 card write: "Adopt Operation 'Fair Share.'" This is a plan where everyone knows they'll get regular pay reviews and their fair share of the company's profits and growth. Establish when pay and performance will be reviewed and the standards and results that can trigger pay and bonuses.

Epilogue

The only way to find out for sure if your people really need the money is to announce that you can't pay them and see how many walk out the door.

128

Correct and Move On

It's a simple truth that of all the loads you will ever carry, the heaviest one to bear is a grudge. Resentment, bitterness, and grudges can dismantle even the best inspirational business environment. Follow the three steps of confront, correct, and move on, and you'll clear the air and remove the tension in your business immediately.

My friend Jerry R. was notorious for being blunt and speaking his mind. At times, his frankness could be very abrasive. But both his friends and employees knew where they stood with him. The best news was that after he vented and got the situation resolved, he never brought it up again. He was the forerunner of confront, correct, and move on.

Assignment

On a 3 × 5 card, write: "When dealing with problems, especially with employees, I will confront them, make appropriate corrections and adjustments, and then move on. Unless it happens again, it's done with and has no bearing on the future."

According to a recent study, 71 percent of all the workers in the United States dread the day as they drive to work. It's not the work they do physically; it's the environment they work in and the attitudes there. Confront, correct, and move on, and you will have a clean-air environment in your place of business. Put the past in the past.

> **Epilogue**
> *When you have a problem, confront it, make corrections, and then move on. And don't go back.*

129

Catch Them Being Good

For reasons no one can clearly understand or explain, human beings are 10 times more likely to find the faults rather than the good in the world. Watch the news media and how the headlines sensationalize life's dark side. It's about murder, mayhem, sex, and scandals. It's easy to fall victim to the negatives and overlook what your people do well. Instead, catch them being good.

Assignment

Write this key phrase on a 3 × 5 card: "Catch them being good." Use this card to remind you that you may have to counsel someone for poor performance, but you also need to reinforce positive performance. That's even more important.

Phil was a frustrated business owner based in Philadelphia. He had tried and tried to get his staff to work as a team and to follow his orders, to no avail. At the end of the day, he went on the attack and was constantly ragging on people and finding their faults. The more he did it, the worse things got. He couldn't understand that when you attack people from the negative you destroy positive behavior. You actually are doing the opposite of what needs to be done to succeed.

Though on occasion you have got to correct people's performance, the secret is finding and acknowledging the 99 things they do right and then having only to correct the one thing you would like them to do better. When you start to criticize, ask yourself, "Does this really matter? Is there a better way of pointing out this person's behavior?"

Epilogue

One more time: what gets rewards gets repeated, and catching people being good is an opportunity to do just that.

130

Focus on Behavior, Not People

There are no bad people, but there are people who have unacceptable behavior. When was the last time someone asked you if you would like to have some constructive criticism? Even if you said yes, I'll bet that you cringed when you heard the negative remarks. No one really likes criticism. When you negatively criticize, it destroys self-esteem.

Bob had a gift to help people improve. He followed three simple steps that you can apply beginning today. When you're confronting behavior problems, the first step is to describe the problem in a friendly manner. The issue while doing that is to protect or enhance self-esteem. Don't let people get down because they see it as criticism. The second step is to ask for their help in solving and resolving the

> **Assignment**
>
> The three-step process of confronting behavior problems is worth committing to a 3 × 5 card: "Describe the problem, then ask their help in resolving the problem, and finally discuss causes and jointly create a plan to fix the behavior." Review as needed.

dilemmas you're discussing. If they won't agree to help and they're not a willing spirit, then you're stuck, and you're going to have to take other action. Step three is to brainstorm possible causes of the problems and then jointly craft a plan to fix it. Remember: self-esteem is more fragile than an egg, and no one likes criticism—even constructive criticism.

Epilogue

Remember to keep any performance review focused on one thing: not the person, but his or her behavior. Protect and enhance his or her self-esteem.

131

Get Mad

Too many business owners would fire someone for stealing quicker than you can say, "Clean out your desk." But then they look the other way when slackers, whiners, and people who undermine productivity and performance get away with it again and again and again. Stealing is stealing, and the worst thieves of all are the ones who blatantly fail to perform in your company. They're stealing the money you need to pay your all-star performers.

Every week, Mae would prepare a pile of payroll checks, and her boss dreaded signing them. And it's not why you think. He truly believed that his best people had earned, deserved, and should get more money for their contributions to the company. He also realized that slackers, whiners, and complainers were stealing—no different than if they were cleaning out the safe. He decided that people who didn't pull their part of their jobs would be offered the opportunity to explore other job opportunities.

> ### Assignment
>
> When you discover slackers eating up your valuable resources and you have been unable to change their behaviors, do what needs to be done and show them the door. On a 3 × 5 card, write: "Slackers are thieves. Discover them and get rid of them." Review as needed.

> ### Epilogue
> *Pay is a by-product; it's the way employees keep score. Get mad when people are stealing from you by giving you substandard performance.*

132

Traditions

One of the reasons people flock to the United States is our rich history and heritage, and the traditions we have in America. From the tradition of celebrating the inauguration of a new president to the tradition of flying the American flag on certain holidays, we are a nation of tradition. You can apply the same logic in your business or organization to inspire, remind, and retain your people. Set up traditions that you do again and again that people will come to love and respect.

Assignment

Get an annual calendar and set up some of the traditions you would like to see in your company. It might be as simple as really and truly decorating for winter holidays to having a traditional annual awards ceremony. Add pomp and circumstance, and make tradition one of the retention tools for your company. Record your planned traditional events on a 3 x 5 card for reference. And remember to involve your team in these events and activities.

Epilogue

People love to celebrate, and today they rarely even get a gold watch. Why not give them a good dose of tradition?

133

I Care and You Matter to Me

Of all the relationships you will have in your life, the most important one is the relationship you have with *you*. And of all the talking you do in your life, the most important conversations are the dialogues you have with yourself—those voices in your head. When you have positive voices and positive talk, you will have positive outcomes, and if you allow negativity to take over, you'll be in big trouble. We need self-talk, and here is a mantra you can adapt.

When Dr. Shad Helmstetter released his book, *What to Say When You Talk to Yourself*, he pointed out that we need an internal dialogue. One that is helpful in business is to adapt the principle of "I care and you matter." When you're confronted with dealing with other people, simply ask yourself, "If I care and they matter, what action should I take?" It will totally change the dialogue you have with yourself.

Assignment

Assignment: To reinforce this principle, write on a 3 × 5 card: "I care and you matter." Review as needed.

Epilogue

When you live by the "I care and you matter" principle, you can make solid changes in your life and use positive thinking to get positive results.

134

Caring and Sharing

If you have tried financial incentive plans to motivate your workforce, it is almost certain you were dismayed or disappointed by the long-term results. All too often such incentive plans take off as shooting stars and then fizzle out as flat tires when you end up rewarding the wrong people. And very often, people get the incentive plans and begin to see them as an entitlement or an expectation.

Virginia-based financial wizard Norm Gaither says most financial incentive plans fail because business owners are paranoid that they might overpay their people. They hedge their bets. They put caps on incentive plans, they set performance standards that can't be met, and they begrudge handing out those incentive checks to employees. Pretty soon, the entire plan fails and they give up. Everyone is disappointed.

Assignment

On a 3 × 5 card, write: "Incentivize by the 50-25-25 plan." Use the card to remind you to set up a incentive program that works. Try it.

Consider a plan where you only incentive or reward people when the company makes a profit. In that manner, you've got everybody working in a team to control expenses and maximize productivity. One formula is called 50-25-25. It's based on net profit after taxes. First, everyone learns that 50 percent of your bottom line profit gets reinvested in the company to buy new equipment, to expand, and to keep up with technology. The second 25 percent of the net profit goes to the shareholders and owners of the company as a cash distribution and a reward for having taken the risk and invested it in the company. Then the final 25 percent gets split among your employees as a percentage of their earned payroll. How can you lose when you only share after-tax profits? And it's a simple, easy-to-understand way that people can see how they can contribute to making the company more profitable.

Epilogue

Consider this incentive plan because it's simple, measurable, and fair. People like it because they can quickly calculate what they will receive.

135

Old Chinese Wisdom

It's pretty difficult to keep people inspired in the long term when they do all the work and owners and management get all the money. Smart management realizes that sharing the profits, if properly planned, can be an investment, not an expense. It can be a tangible way to show people that their performance is needed and that their success can pay off in a personal way.

There's an old Chinese proverb that says, "When you drink the water, don't forget the people that helped you dig the well." Sometimes even modest cash distributions can trigger a sense of pride and enthusiasm that

Assignment

On a 3 × 5 card, write: "Cash rewards for performance work when they are applied judiciously and occasionally." Use this card to remind you that occasional cash rewards as incentive do work when they are justified and when they don't become an expectation.

can be contagious throughout your company. Such cash distributions, when coupled with positive feedback, can keep your company fired up on all eight cylinders seven days a week.

Epilogue

Remember that, by sharing the wealth, your workers will end up helping you make more.

136

Nothing to Hide; Hide Nothing

We've seen it again and again. All too many owners and managers are paranoid that their workforce might find out about the company's finances. They don't want them to know how much profit they earned, probably thinking they will ask for a raise. Company finances become a deep, dark secret, and management plays games to withhold information from their workforce.

Assignment

It doesn't need to be a deep dark secret. Write on a 3 × 5 card: "Let everyone know how we make money (or measure success). Once they know, they'll be in a better position to help."

When Sears Roebuck hired a new CEO, he quickly became concerned that his workforce misunderstood profit, mark-up, and what Sears truly makes when they make a sale. He did a survey, and asked the employees, "How much do you think Sears earns as a profit after all expenses and taxes, when we make a one-dollar sale?" The least amount that was handed in was two cents, and the highest amount was $1.10. He had confirmed his fear: there was a gross misunderstanding about profits, and Sears set about to educate its workforce so they would be better attuned to helping Sears make money.

There's an old saying: people who are given information can't help but take responsibility for it, and people who are not given information cannot take responsibility. If you have nothing to hide, hide nothing. Put the finances out where everyone can see them, and everyone will be better off.

Epilogue

Eighty percent of your workforce believes you make more profits than you actually do, and 20 percent probably believe you're lying to them.

137

Test Question: Am I Fairly Paid?

If you interviewed 1,700 workers in all segments of business across the United States and asked the question, "Do you feel that you are fairly paid?" how many do you think would answer yes? How many would say, "No, I deserve more money"? The answer might surprise you, and what people really want from you is to know that you will be fair.

I've actually done this survey. And in all of the people I asked, only three said they felt they were underpaid! What people really want to know is this: If they contribute to the company's success, and the company makes more money, will management recognize them and share the wealth? Will they get their raises when appropriate? Will they get their share of

Assignment

"I will make sure that I reassure my team they will be rewarded with their 'fair share.' And I will make certain that actually happens." Write that statement on a 3 × 5 card. Review it occasionally to remind you that "fair share" is more important that actual salary or wages with employees.

profits when they should? Again, their main question is, "Will I get my fair share?"

Adopt the idea that you have a fair share program. Let people know when there's money to be divided, and explain how you've gone about figuring it out. Let them know that they will get their fair share no matter what.

Epilogue

You can tell people about your fair share program again and again, but when you distribute the money, they will know you mean business and trust you in the future.

138

Beware of the Seniority Trap

In the past, the tradition in American business was that for each year you stayed with a company, you got more money. It didn't take all that many years for management to learn they had been trapped. It didn't result in more productive people; it just meant they'd hung around longer. Why should that deserve more money? Why shouldn't people be paid for their performance?

When a group of Minneapolis retail stores got in deep trouble because their payroll was grossly out of line as a percentage of sales, they had to make some drastic changes. Over the years, some of their senior people had gotten raise after raise, and it had gotten away from them. They had to completely replace their pay plan with a lesser hourly amount coupled with an incentive program. The incentive program provided that when they made sales and profit goals, people got their shares. Beware of handing out money just because someone's been hanging around. They may be your least productive workers.

Assignment

"More seniority does not mean more productivity. I'm going to create a meritocracy and pay people based on performance, not longevity." Write this on a 3 × 5 card. Now create a new pay plan that reflects performance, not time-in-service.

Epilogue

Tom Peters, a famous author and consultant, believes that 40 percent of someone's take-home pay should be based on incentives, thus avoiding the seniority trap. Consider that formula for yourself.

139

Rank Has Its Privileges

Have you ever felt guilty because you followed the free enterprise system in America and made it pay off for you? Have you ever felt guilty because perhaps you have a better

Assignment

"RHIP (Rank Has Its Privileges) is not a four-letter word." Write that on a 3 × 5 card and pull it out to review the next time someone tries to make you feel guilty because of what you have earned.

home than your neighbor, more money than someone who works for you, or a better car than someone else? If so, you need to remind yourself that earned rank has its privileges.

Once again, to understand this principle, we look at the United States military. As people move up the ranks, from private to, perhaps, sergeant, to lieutenant, to colonel, and clear on up to General, they enjoy more privileges. They also have more responsibilities, more worries, and more work. The president of the United States gets to fly on Air Force One. Rank has its privileges. Think about the risks you have taken, the investments you have made, the hours you have worked, the education you have sweated to gain, and the many times you've been working while others are out playing. You've paid a dear price for your success and you should enjoy it. Simply remind yourself that rank has its privileges, and if you've earned it honestly and legitimately, enjoy it. If other people are envious of you, feel sorry for them. Tell him they can get it the old-fashioned way. They can work for it.

Epilogue

When you think about this idea, remember that America is the greatest free country in the world because every man, woman, and child has the equal right to be unequal.

140

Want Loyalty?
Get Yourself a Dog!

All too often, people in leadership positions believe their employees should be loyal just because they gave them a job and they pay them for what they do. Loyalty is something you earn, not something you are owed. You get it by providing both the basics and the extras over a long period of time. Loyalty must be earned. There's no other way to get it.

When Cindy's boss got a memo from her, he noticed a Post-it note attached to it that said, "If you want loyalty, get a dog. I work for money." His immediate thought was that this was a plea for more money. Was he underpaying Cindy? When he confronted her, they both had a good laugh, because it was simply something she had found and thought he would get a chuckle from it. But it made an indelible point that he will never forget. People do need money to buy the things that they need in life, and when you fail to pay them appropriately, you not only lose their loyalty, you lose them as employees.

> ### Assignment
>
> On a 3 × 5 card, write: "If you want loyalty, get a dog." Use this card to remind yourself that people give loyalty only if it is earned. Go earn it.

> ### Epilogue
> *All too often, people in leadership positions want loyalty despite the fact that they don't want to pay an adequate amount of money and offer the fringe benefit programs people deserve.*

141

Control Benefits Costs by Measuring and Monitoring P&L Creep

Isn't it amazing how overhead expenses can inch ahead, and you really miss the fact that not only do they cost more money, but they're consuming an increasing percentage of your profit and loss statement? One of the smart things managers do is to compare overhead items, such as fringe benefits, liability insurance, and workman's comp insurance, as a percentage of their gross sales. That way you can know what the percentage was last month, and you can watch that it doesn't escalate month after month. It's easy to ignore when such an expense becomes 2 percent of your gross, then 2 1/2 percent, then 3 percent, then 3 1/2 percent.

All expenses, from benefits to rent to payroll, should be looked at as a percentage of your gross sales. When gross sales go up, you have more money to invest in those expense items. The primary thing is to watch out for the creep, because it'll slip up on you and bite you right in the wallet.

Assignment

"Watch out for that creep!" Write that on a 3 × 5 card and review it monthly to remind you to calculate your overhead as a percentage of gross sales and run a month-to-month comparison. Keep control of "creep" and you will end up with more cash available to reinvest in your key assets: your employees.

Epilogue

People who say money's not important should try doing without it.

142

Show Me the Money

Cuba Gooding, Jr., coined the phrase "show me the money" in the movie *Jerry Maguire*. That philosophy can be fun if you want to use cash for some contest, incentive plans, or the opportunity for people to earn extra income. Consider getting some big bills—for example, $100—and put them on a bulletin board or lock them up in a glass case, but leave them where everybody can see them. There's something exciting about that long green with a president's picture on it.

Each morning, Mary Ann, the sales coordinator for a large manufacturing company, would get a stack of money from the safe and during their morning sales meeting she would methodically sit there and count it. There were several thousand

---

Assignment

"Show me the money!" Write that on a card to remind you that doing just that can be motivating.

---

dollars that would be handed out at the end of the month for the salespeople who performed according to the company's incentive plan. She was "showing them the money," and reminding them that the incentives would be paid off on the 30th of the month in cold, hard cash. The plan worked, and everybody got some money, and some people got a lot of money. But everybody enjoyed her "showing the money." And guess what else happened? Sales went up!

> ### Epilogue
>
> *There's something almost mystical and magical about cash, and "showing people the money" can be an incentive in ways that the promise of a check never will. Try it.*

143

Behavior = Outcomes

American management continues to make a lot of errors, and one of the most tragic ones is when they become focused on the activity and not the outcomes they want to accomplish. Employees get confused when they get mixed messages about what the company wants to accomplish—when on a day-by-day basis, everything is about the activities and what's going on in the company. We lose sight of what we're really trying to accomplish. Noted management consultant Peter Drucker says, "The purpose of a business should be to cultivate a following of customers."

When discussing the behavior you would like to have

> ### Assignment
>
> "Activities vs. Outcomes? I want outcomes." Write this on a 3 × 5 card and use it occasionally to remind you that when you talk to your team about their "activities," what you are going to measure—and value—is outcomes.

from your people, relate everything in terms of outcomes and what you're really trying to accomplish, which is to serve the customer. The goal is not to get the customer today. You've probably already accomplished that. The objective should be to get customers back one more time to give you another opportunity to sell them and serve them. When you discuss what you expect from your employees, always relate it to the end result you're looking for and why it is important to customers. If you don't get repeat business, you're going to spend all your time looking for new customers, and your costs will go through the roof.

Epilogue

Activities make us feel good, but outcomes make us money. Keep your eye on what's important, and that's having customers who will buy again and again.

144

1 More Time: Me to We

Is your company infected by a bad case of individualism? Do you have internal competition to see what each individual can do and how each can outperform the other? If you do, those are very destructive traits, because we know that success is a team sport. The United States military has proven that teamwork must be the goal of all training and activities. If you don't have teamwork, you're wasting a lot of manpower.

There's probably no better example of changing "me" to "we" than to watch NASCAR racing. When one car is alone out on the track, trying to cut its way through the air at high speed, it's a challenge. When a second car comes up behind that one and they team up, the second car gets in the draft and it accelerates both cars. It has become so important that partnerships in NASCAR are essential. Teamwork is a must. The very definition of teamwork—TEAM (Together Everyone Accomplishes More)—should be the goal of your business or organization.

Assignment

Write on a 3 × 5 card: "TEAM (Together Everyone Accomplishes More): We is more powerful than Me." Use this card weekly to remind yourself to build a team and not to create individual high performers alone.

Be forewarned that a group of people working together is not teamwork. Teamwork is when the collective group sublimates their individual needs to the team and the team ends up producing more than the same group of individuals would.

Epilogue

The goal is to change "me" to "we," and it's an ever-present challenge, as most people think of the Big Three (Me, Myself, and I). Don't ever give up on teamwork.

145

Your Definition of Success

How do you and your people measure company success? What kind of yardstick do you use to define winning? There are many ways, from gross revenue to market share to net profit. But the important point is to have a clear, definable, and measurable goal, a goal that everybody knows and can understand. How would you know if a quarterback was moving the ball if the field lacked yard lines, hash marks, and the goal post?

At one time, John Paul Getty, the oil czar, was one of the wealthiest men in the world. When asked, "How much is enough money?" His response was, "Just a little bit more." All too often, business owners follow that same logic: "We need a little bit more." But they fail to share the yardstick for everyone to see. People don't really know where they're going because no one has communicated the

Assignment

On a 3 × 5 card, write: "What is our definition of success? How do we measure it? Does my team know what that goal is?" This card should be reviewed weekly to make certain you have identified a measurable goal and that you have shared that goal with your team.

goal to them. When a definition of success is not shared with your team, they never get to savor the thrill of victory, either personally or professionally.

At the end of the day, people want to believe that they work for an organization that cares about them. They want to participate in something more than just making money. They want to leave the world better than they found it, and they want a measurable system so they know when they have won.

Epilogue

There's nothing more degrading than to constantly be told, "We need just a little bit more," but not knowing the goal.

146

Your Inspiration = Their Perspiration

The ripple effect of a leader's inspiration, enthusiasm, and optimism is awesome. So is the impact of cynicism and pessimism. Leaders who whine and blame spread the same behaviors among their colleagues. I'm talking about not blindly accepting organizational stupidity, poor performance, or lack of competence with a "What, me? Worry?" attitude. I'm talking about a gung-ho attitude that says, "We can change things here. We can achieve awesome goals. We can be the best. We're going to be the best."

Dr. Robert Schuller tells a story of 12 randomly picked people brought into the company conference room and told they'd been handpicked to resolve a special problem. They were told that they had a gift, and that's why they were picked. The group went to work. The inspiration of being handpicked, and the story they were told, equaled their perspiration and, lo and behold, guess what happened? They resolved the problem effectively. Never give up on inspiration, enthusiasm, and optimism. Perpetual optimism is a force multiplier.

Assignment

"The power of the positive attitude is infectious." Write this on a 3 × 5 card. Review it daily. Consider posting it as a sign or poster in the workspace to help inspire others.

Epilogue

Remember the adage, "If it is to be, it is up to me." And that is so true with inspiration.

147

Technology Requires Investment

Has it hit you that the future is where you will spend the rest of your life? And has it soaked in that technology is driving change at warp speed? Just keeping pace requires monitoring the landscape 24/7. Simply assessing where you need to invest to maintain a competitive reputation is a job all in itself.

A Las Vegas printing company has a philosophy that any time a new piece of equipment, from a computer to a printing press, is introduced they immediately check it out to see if it's significantly better than the one they currently use. If it will increase their productivity and/or their quality, they immediately buy the new equipment and sell the old, even though their old may be only months old. There are always willing buyers. The

Assignment

Set up a budget for automatically investing in new technology. Have a task force within your company to monitor it so it's not a one-person job. To remind you of this, on a 3 × 5 card, write: "Adopting early technology leads to better business, more profits, and better employees. I support this idea."

point? This company has a reputation for producing state-of-the-art quality printing, unlike many other printing companies. And what work do they get as a result? State-of-the-art, highest quality from companies that are willing to pay a little more because they know this company has the best equipment in the world.

What does this mean for your team? If you are on the cutting edge, they will be too. And they'll know it and be inspired about it because it sets them apart from the competition just as it sets your company apart.

Epilogue

Henry Ford said, "If you need a tool and you don't buy it, you will end up paying for it and never get to use it."

148

Sort Ideas: Today, Tomorrow, and the Future

Looking into the future can often be overwhelming. In time management and productivity, there's an old saying: "How do you eat an elephant?" The answer is "one bite at a time." Many people have said that by breaking a project down into bites, anyone can handle it.

One highly respected consultant had a habit of overwhelming his clients. He would do what he called a "business analysis" and create for them a roadmap into the future. However, all too often the roadmap became so overwhelming that people just wanted to throw up their hands and give up.

He learned that the way to present his ideas was to offer them in phases: Here are the things we want to do today. Here are the things we will work on tomorrow. And here are the things we might work on in the future. By doing that, people found the

Assignment

"How do you eat an elephant? One bite at a time!" Write this on a 3 × 5 card to remind you not to overwhelm your team with new ideas and work, but to parcel it out in digestible pieces.

196

ideas more easily digestible. Think about breaking down what you plan to do into some format where you can phase it in and not overwhelm people.

Epilogue

There's a hidden benefit in selling the future, because it offers people a view that you've got a clear blueprint on where to go. The by-product is that they end up with hope, optimism, and inspiration for the future.

149

How to Fire People and Have Them Say Thank You

One of the most unpleasant tasks all managers must undertake from time to time is firing someone. Many a manager has walked the floor all night or has become extremely nauseated at the very thought of having to confront and fire a worker. If you've experienced that kind of anxiety, then you have proven you are human. Good for you.

When Stan joined a company that required a lot of interaction with customers in helping them diagnose and solve their problems, he immediately began to struggle with the issues involved. As the weeks went by, he tried and tried, but it was painfully obvious that Stan was not cut out for the job. As his supervisor began to counsel him, they got to the bottom of the issue: Stan was just not a people person, and he really didn't want to do the job he had been assigned. The supervisor, being very savvy, encouraged Stan to explore other employment and

Assignment

On a 3 × 5 card (still have some?), write: "Let them go easy, but let them go. You're helping the organization, the team, and the individual." Review this card every time you are faced with the prospect of firing someone.

even helped him get a job as a bricklayer. Stan actually thanked that supervisor.

When you know someone's not a fit and you allow him or her to stay on, you're hurting both the employee and the company. Let him or her down easy, but help the person realize that he or she just doesn't fit. That does not make him or her a bad person. Encourage the person to move on because it's hurting *his or her* future.

Epilogue

Regardless of how hard you try, some people are just not going to fit in your organization. Never hurt people when they have to exit your company.

150

Applause: Your To-Done List

Are you a to-do list maker? Are you someone who prefers to have a working agenda on paper, in your computer, or perhaps on your PDA? Then you realize your to-do list is rarely caught up, and every time you get something accomplished, something pops up to take its place. Will you ever get caught up? Do you find that to-do list overwhelming and kind of a grind?

Imagine for a moment that you were elected president of the United States. You would surely have a to-do list, even though someone else might keep it for you. Never is a president elected to solve all of our problems, get finished, turn the lights out, and go home. Our president, much in that same way

> ## Assignment
>
> *"To Do* and *To Done."* Put that on a 3 × 5 card. Now, every month review your *To Done* list to see just how much you have accomplished. Require all of your employees to do the same.

that you are, is elected to work on the issues that come up and the projects he or she takes on, and it seems to be a never-ending assembly line. It's got to be an incredibly overwhelming job, just as yours is some days.

Consider keeping your to-do list for a week or a month or maybe even a year, and use it as a scorecard. Look backwards to have a to-*done* list and analyze all of the things you have accomplished. It can make you realize that your to-do list works, and it can also be a pat on the back for all of the things you are getting accomplished. It will change your attitude and it will make you look into the future with a smile that will inspire everyone around you. Get your team members to do the same thing. It's actually quite inspiring.

> ### Epilogue
> *A to-done list is a necessity for management because rarely are you going to get a pat on the back from someone else, and you have to learn the art of self-congratulations. Give yourself some applause.*

151

Buy My Books and Use Them

Congratulations! If you've worked all 151 quick ideas, hopefully you've identified perhaps the top, three, five, or 10 ideas that you should begin to implement today, but there's one more action step that is critical if you're going to get the maximum payoff from this book.

Buy a book for each of your employees. You might challenge them to pick their top three or five or 10 and, as a group, decide which of those would give you the biggest payoff in the least amount of time, with the least effort, starting right now.

If you see books and ideas as an investment, you will want to buy them for all your people. It's a small price to pay, because one quick idea could pay off significantly.

Assignment

Okay, you've created enough 3 × 5 cards. Now do three things with them:

1. Pick some specific, quick ideas to implement.
2. Turn these into a contest or spoofs or campaign or competitions.
3. Have fun implementing some quick ideas that will reap quick results.

Epilogue

Remember that you invest in a book just once, but you get to use the quick ideas forever. Think of it as making a very small deposit and getting paid interest every day.

Index

About the Author

Twenty-five years ago, when Jerry Wilson began his professional career managing one small auto parts store, it would have been hard to imagine that he would become a world-renowned expert in marketing and develop a new marketing and customer retention philosophy called Customerology.

Yet that is just what happened. Jerry grew his small auto parts store into an extremely profitable retail store group that dominated the area in which it was located. Not content with simply increasing sales in his own business, Jerry leveraged and expanded this experience, soon becoming well known for his retail store operations and sales and management consulting.

Jerry was also the author of the highly acclaimed *Word-of-Mouth Marketing, 138 Quick Ideas to Get More Clients*, and *How to Grow Your Auto Parts Business*, published in numerous languages and distributed internationally. Jerry also authored more than 100 feature articles on customer retention for a variety of association and industry trade journals in both the United States and Canada.

As a result of his experiences, Jerry developed a new "science"—Customerology—to aid companies in gaining and retaining satisfied customers. As a consultant, Jerry assisted such companies as Firestone, Merchants Tire, Stanley Publishing, and Ripley's Believe It Or Not, helping them rethink customer philosophies, service strategies, and practices. Jerry also served as executive director for a large state trade association and consulted with business leaders on national and international levels.

For example, in New Zealand, Jerry worked hand-in-hand with management to overhaul Rainbow's End Theme Park after its rescue from bankruptcy. After revamping its customer relations system in accord with Jerry's advice, the theme park realized a 70,000-attendee increase over the previous year—quantifiable success as a result of the tenets of Customerology.

At Merchant's Tire, a 100-plus chain of tire and auto service stores based in Virginia, Jerry assisted management with a campaign to reduce customer complaints. After implementing the Customerology system, the chain saw customer complaints plummet more than 50 percent.

These astounding successes led to numerous speaking engagements for Jerry Wilson. As a professional speaker, Jerry appeared before more than 1,000 groups and traveled to all 50 states, as well as Canada, New Zealand, Indonesia, and South America. His keynote presentations, seminars, and workshops benefited countless companies and organizations worldwide.

Jerry was awarded the Certified Speaking Professional (CSP) designation by the National Speakers Association, a prestigious award given to only 400 speakers worldwide. He served two terms as president of the Indiana chapter of the National Speakers Association and also served as chair of the NSA's CSP Certification Committee.

Jerry was honored by being listed in the *Who's Who Directory of the Midwest* and in the *World Directory of Men of Achievement*.